The Secret Patriots

Hidden Heroes Who Shaped America When It Mattered Most

BOOK 1: WAR AND POWER

GRANT WHITMORE

Copyright © 2025 by HMDPublishing

All rights are reserved, and no part of this publication may be reproduced, distributed, or transmitted in any manner, whether through photocopying, recording, or any other electronic or mechanical methods, without the explicit prior written permission of the publisher. This restriction applies to any form or means of reproduction or distribution.

Exceptions to this rule include brief quotations that may be incorporated into critical reviews, as well as certain other noncommercial uses that are allowed by copyright law. Any such usage must adhere to the specified conditions and permissions outlined by the copyright holder.

Book Design by HMDPublishing.com

Contents

Introduction: The Real America Lives in the Shadows 5

Part 1
The Women Who Fought Back

Chapter 1   The Limping Lady Who Terrorized Hitler 19
Chapter 2   America's Secret Army Wore Lipstick 37
Chapter 3   The Price of Victory 61

Part 2
Patriots You Never Heard Of

Chapter 4   The Other Midnight Ride 87
Chapter 5   The Slave Who Spied for Freedom 117
Chapter 6   Lincoln's Other Right Hand 145
Chapter 7   The Man Who Organized a Dream 179
Chapter 8   The Mother of a Movement 209

Part 3
The Crucible of Power: Presidential Leadership in Crisis

Chapter 9   Lincoln's Rhetorical Genius 239
Chapter 10   FDR's Triple Crisis 267
Chapter 11   The President Nobody Expected to Lead 293

Part 4
The Hidden Truth About American Courage

Chapter 12   What Makes a Hero? 325
Chapter 13   The Heroes Among Us 347

Prologue 381
Epilogue: The Real American Story 385

Introduction: The Real America Lives in the Shadows

Figure 1: Echoes of courage in the shadows of history

History lied to you.

Not intentionally, perhaps, but the America you learned about in textbooks, the one carved in marble monuments and celebrated in Fourth of July parades, tells only half the story. That version of history focuses on the obvious heroes: the generals who won famous battles, the presidents whose faces grace currency, the founding fathers whose signatures appear on parchment under museum glass.

But the real America, the one that actually shaped our national character and secured our freedoms, was built by people whose names you've never heard. Their stories live in the shadows of our collective memory, buried beneath decades of convenient narratives that celebrate the comfortable and ignore the complicated.

Consider this: While Paul Revere gets credit for his midnight ride, a sixteen-year-old girl named Sybil Ludington rode twice as far through enemy territory on the same mission. While celebrating the Founding Fathers, we forget James Armistead Lafayette, an enslaved man who risked everything to spy for Washington while fighting for his own freedom. While we honor the March on Washington, we overlook Bayard Rustin, the brilliant strategist who organized every detail but couldn't march in the front row because he was gay.

These aren't footnotes to American history. They *are* American history.

INTRODUCTION: THE REAL AMERICA LIVES IN THE SHADOWS

THE HEROES WHO HID IN PLAIN SIGHT

> **DEPARTMENT OF STATE**
> WASHINGTON
>
> November 26, 1937
>
> Miss Virginia Hall
> Baltimore, Maryland
>
> My dear Miss Hall:
>
> I regret to have to advise you that the oficials of the Department, including the Office of the Chief Examiner of the Civil Service Commission, after an analysis of your recent examination, have- ▉.
>
> The fact that you corrected your ▉- has caused me to believe that you had high ▉.
>
> Yours sincerely,

> **O.S.S.:**
> Washington, D. C.
> 16 September 1945
>
> VIRGINIA HALL, Mrs.,
>
> For exemplary performance of duty in the field. As an organizer, inspiration and leader of resistance forces, Mrs. HALL was more than deserving or ▉, Her arduous preparatory work and perfect timing made possible the ▉ played in the recapture of ▉ - will reflect great credit to herself and to the O.S.S.

Figure 2: From rejection to resistance: the classified rise of Virginia Hall.

Take Virginia Hall, who lost her leg in a hunting accident and was told by the State Department that she was "unsuitable for foreign service." Instead of accepting that verdict, she became America's most effective spy in Nazi-occupied France. The Gestapo called her "the most dangerous of all Allied spies" and put a bounty on her head. She organized resistance networks, coordinated sabotage operations, and saved countless Allied lives, all while walking on a wooden leg she nicknamed "Cuthbert."

Virginia Hall quietly returned to America when the war ended and took a desk job with the newly formed CIA. No parades welcomed her home. No monuments honored her service. She lived the rest of her life in suburban anonymity, her wartime exploits classified for decades. The woman who had terrorized the Third Reich spent her golden years tending to her garden in Maryland.

Why don't you know her name?

The answer reveals something uncomfortable about how we choose our heroes. We prefer our patriots simple, our narratives clean, our courage conventional. We celebrate the obvious acts of bravery, the charge up San Juan Hill, the crossing of the Delaware, while ignoring the messy, complicated, and often inconvenient courage that actually holds a democracy together.

THE UNCOMFORTABLE TRUTH ABOUT COURAGE

Figure 3: Two legacies stitched into history — one in marble, one in thread.

Real courage rarely looks like what Hollywood taught us to expect. It doesn't wear a uniform or carry a flag. It doesn't make speeches or pose for paintings. Instead, it shows up in quiet moments when ordinary people make extraordinary choices that no one will ever thank them for.

Elizabeth Keckley understood this kind of courage. Born into slavery, she bought her own freedom through her skill as a seamstress, then used that same skill to dress Mary Todd Lincoln during the Civil War's darkest hours. As the First Lady's confidante, Keckley had unprecedented access to power during America's greatest crisis. She could have used that access for personal gain. Instead, she spent her own money to organize relief efforts for freed slaves and counseled the president's wife through the deaths of their son and, eventually, her husband.

Keckley lived at the intersection of slavery and freedom, powerlessness and influence, anonymity and access. Her story complicates our understanding of who held real power during the Civil War and who deserves credit for healing a divided nation. But complicated stories don't fit easily on commemorative coins or in elementary school textbooks, so we remember Lincoln and forget the woman who helped him carry the weight of a broken country.

THE PATTERN HIDDEN IN PLAIN SIGHT

Figure 4: In every American crisis, a hidden hero stood quietly in the fire.

Once you start looking for these hidden patriots, you begin to see a pattern that runs through every major crisis in American history. When the nation faces its darkest moments, when democracy itself hangs in the balance, the people who step forward to save it are rarely the ones you'd expect.

They're often outsiders: women in a man's world, minorities in a white majority, the disabled in an ableist society, the marginalized fighting for the mainstream that rejects them. They're people who understand what it means to be underestimated, overlooked, and undervalued. And perhaps because they know what it feels like to be written off, they refuse to write off their country, even when their country has written them off.

During World War II, while men went off to fight the obvious war on foreign soil, women fought a secret war in occupied territory and government offices. During the Civil Rights era, while charismatic leaders gave stirring speeches, behind-the-scenes organizers built the infrastructure that actually moved mountains. During moments of presidential crisis, while the nation looked for perfect leaders, flawed human beings found ways to rise to impossible occasions.

This pattern isn't an accident. It reveals something fundamental about how democracy actually works. The people most invested in saving American ideals are often those who have been denied the full benefits of American citizenship. They fight hardest for the dream because they understand its cost better than anyone.

WHY THESE STORIES MATTER NOW

Figure 5: They don't wear capes—just purpose, grit, and quiet resolve.

We live in another moment when American democracy faces existential threats. Political polarization has reached levels not seen since the

Civil War. Trust in institutions has collapsed. The very idea of shared truth seems like a relic from a simpler time. In moments like these, it's tempting to look backward and imagine that previous generations had it easier, that their heroes were more heroic, their choices more clear-cut.

But that's exactly backward. Every generation of Americans has faced moments when the country's survival seemed uncertain, when the gap between American ideals and American reality felt unbridgeable, when ordinary citizens had to choose between comfortable silence and dangerous action. The people who chose action, who stepped forward when stepping forward was costly, didn't do it because they were saints or geniuses or natural-born leaders.

They did it because someone had to.

Virginia Hall didn't become a spy because she was fearless. She was terrified every day she operated behind enemy lines. Elizabeth Keckley didn't become Lincoln's confidante because she was power-hungry. She was a formerly enslaved woman who understood that proximity to power came with responsibility. Bayard Rustin didn't organize the March on Washington because he craved recognition. He knew his sexuality would make him a liability, but he also knew the march was more important than his personal comfort.

These people became heroes not despite their vulnerabilities, but because of them. Their outsider status gave them clarity about what was worth fighting for. Their personal experience with injustice motivated them to ensure others wouldn't suffer the same fate. Their intimate knowledge of what America could be, rather than what it was, drove them to bridge that gap through individual action.

THE HIDDEN THREAD

Figure 6: Threads of time, woven by unseen hands into the fabric of our freedom

What connects a disabled spy in Nazi-occupied France, an enslaved patriot in Revolutionary Virginia, and a gay organizer in the Jim Crow South? What links a seamstress in Lincoln's White House with teenage girls riding through the night to save the colonial militia? What ties together presidents making impossible decisions in the White House with ordinary citizens making extraordinary choices in their communities?

The answer isn't complicated, even if the stories are. They all understood that democracy isn't a spectator sport. They all recognized that freedom isn't free, not in the sense that someone else pays the price, but in the sense that every generation must earn it again. They all grasped that the distance between American ideals and American reality would only be closed by people willing to do the closing, one difficult decision at a time.

Most importantly, they all realized that waiting for someone else to save the country meant the country wouldn't be saved.

The heroes in this book didn't set out to become heroes. They set out to solve problems, right wrongs, and serve something larger than themselves. They became heroes because heroism is what happens when ordinary people make extraordinary choices in ordinary moments. And in America, those moments come more often than we'd like to admit.

YOUR INHERITANCE

Figure 7: A modern American flag, slightly worn, flying against a dawn sky

This book isn't just about the past. It's about recognizing that the same spirit that drove Virginia Hall to limp through Nazi-occupied France, that inspired James Armistead Lafayette to risk everything for a country that enslaved him, that motivated Ella Baker to organize a movement from the shadows, that spirit still exists today.

It exists in the teacher who stays late to help struggling students, knowing she won't get credit or extra pay. It lives in the community organizer who builds bridges between divided neighborhoods, understanding that the work is slow and the recognition rare. It shows up in the citizen who speaks truth to power, even when truth-telling comes with consequences.

The secret patriots of American history weren't superhuman. They were supremely human, flawed, frightened, uncertain people who found ways to act courageously when courage was required. They made mistakes, suffered defeats, and sometimes paid terrible prices for their choices. But they chose to act rather than watch, to participate rather than complain, to build rather than tear down.

Their stories matter because they prove that heroism isn't reserved for special people in special times. It's available to anyone willing to step forward when stepping forward is needed. And in America, stepping forward is always needed.

The real America lives in the shadows of our official history, waiting to be discovered by each new generation. These are the stories of the people who built that America, not with marble and bronze, but with moral courage and stubborn hope. They are your inheritance, your inspiration, and your challenge.

The question isn't whether you're worthy of their example. The question is whether you're willing to follow it.

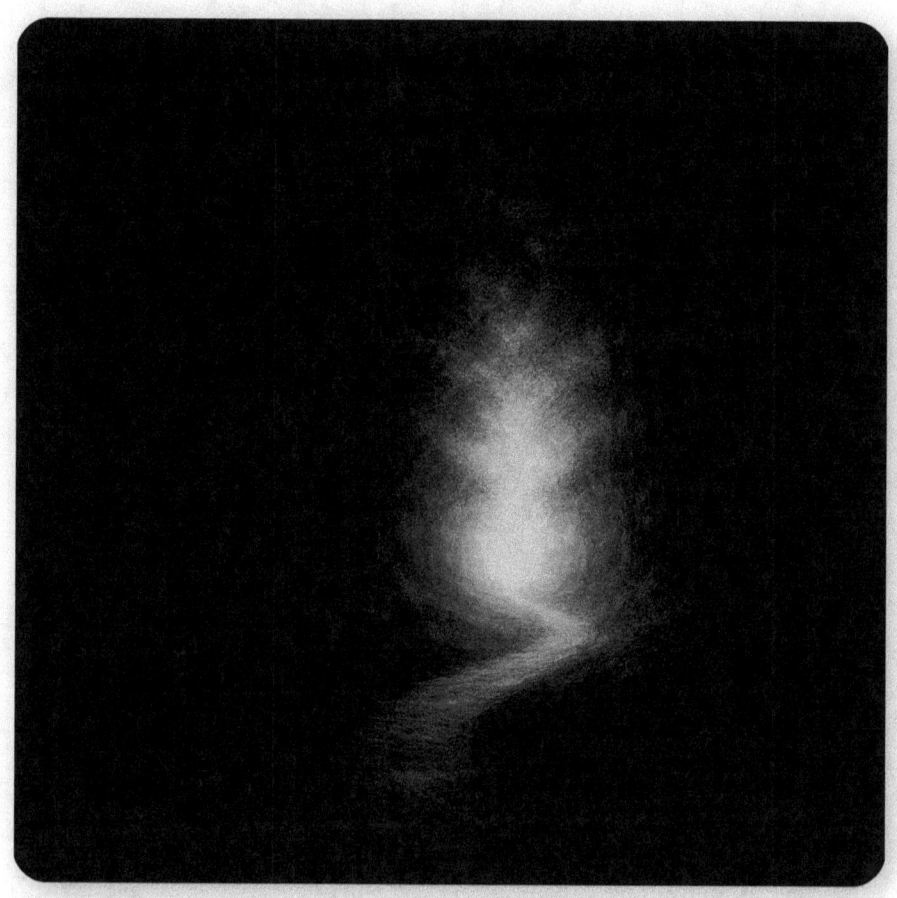

Figure 8: Every step forward brings truth out of the shadows.

Part I:
The Women Who Fought Back

When the world was burning, they lit the fuse

Chapter 1:
The Limping Lady Who Terrorized Hitler

VIRGINIA HALL'S WAR AGAINST THE THIRD REICH

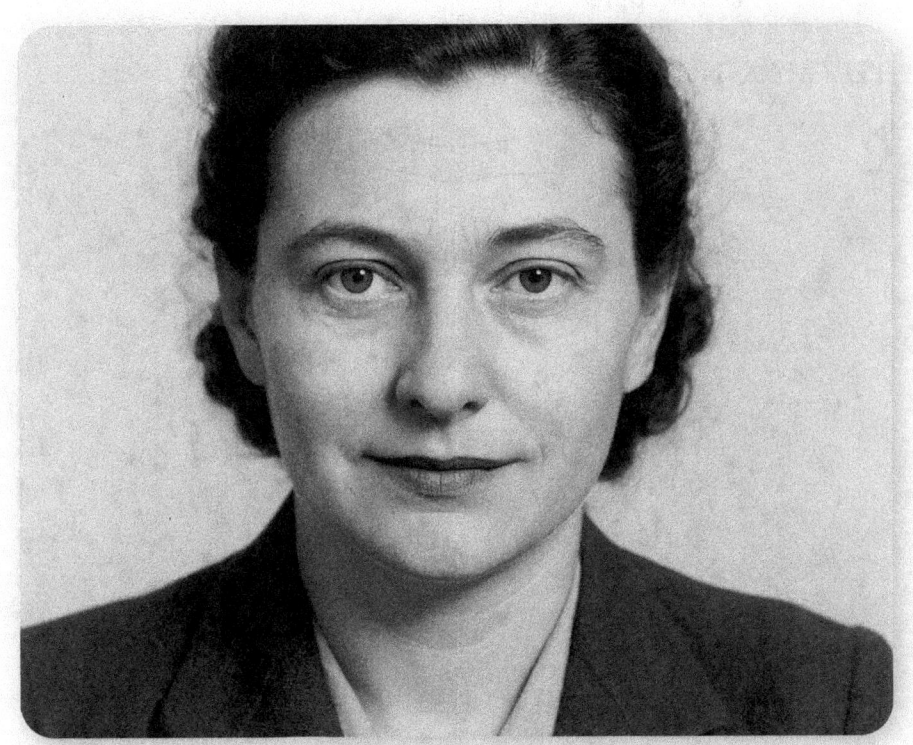

Figure 9: The unassuming face that outwitted the Nazis and became their most feared Allied spy

The rejection letter was polite but final. "Miss Hall," it read, "while we appreciate your interest in foreign service, your recent injury makes you unsuitable for overseas assignment." The date was 1931. Virginia Hall was twenty-five years old, brilliant, and fluent in French, German, and Italian. She was also missing her left leg below the knee, the result of a hunting accident in Turkey that had ended her dreams of a diplomatic career before they began.

The State Department's loss would become Hitler's nightmare.

Most people would have accepted that verdict and found a different path. Virginia Hall was not like most people. Tall, striking, and possessed of what friends called "an iron will wrapped in velvet gloves," she refused to let other people's limitations become her limitations. If America wouldn't let her serve her country officially, she'd find another way.

She had no idea that "another way" would make her the most wanted woman in Nazi-occupied Europe.

THE MAKING OF A SPY

Figure 10: In the cafés of Paris, she found freedom stitched into every cup and conversation

Virginia Hall didn't set out to become a spy. Born in Baltimore in 1906 to a well-to-do family, she was the kind of young woman who was expected to marry well and host dinner parties, not organize resistance networks and coordinate prison breaks. But Hall had always been different. She excelled in school, played basketball and baseball, and showed an early fascination with languages and foreign cultures.

After her accident and the State Department's rejection, she did what many well-educated young Americans did in the 1930s: she went to Paris. The City of Light was a magnet for ambitious Americans seeking adventure and sophistication they couldn't find at home. Hall enrolled at the École Libre des Sciences Politiques, perfected her French, and tried to figure out what to do with her life.

She was still figuring it out when German tanks rolled into Poland in September 1939.

Hall could have returned home like many European Americans when war broke out. Instead, she moved closer to the danger. She found work with the American Embassy in London, helping coordinate evacuations and refugee assistance. The work was meaningful but frustrating; she wanted to do more than process paperwork while Europe burned.

Her opportunity came from an unexpected source: the British Special Operations Executive, or SOE. Created by Winston Churchill with the mandate to "set Europe ablaze," the SOE was recruiting agents to work behind enemy lines in occupied territory. They needed people who spoke perfect French, could blend in with local populations, and had the courage to operate in constant danger.

Virginia Hall was perfect, except for one obvious problem.

"How will you explain the limp?" asked the SOE officer conducting her interview.

Hall's answer revealed the quick thinking that would keep her alive for the next four years: "I'll tell them I was injured in an Allied bombing raid. It will make me a more convincing victim of the war."

The British were convinced. In August 1941, Virginia Hall crossed the English Channel and entered Nazi-occupied France. Her cover story was simple: she was an American journalist working for the New York Post, filing stories about life under German occupation. Her real mission was far more dangerous: to organize French resistance fighters, coordinate sabotage operations, and gather intelligence for the Allied war effort.

She had no formal espionage training, experience with clandestine operations, or backup plan if things went wrong. What she had was something the Germans would learn to fear: an absolute refusal to accept defeat.

THE LIMPING LADY'S FIRST NETWORK

Figure 11: Lyon, the nerve center of a silent war—her routes, their freedom

Hall established her base of operations in Lyon, the largest city in unoccupied Vichy France. Officially, the Vichy government collaborated with the Germans. Unofficially, Lyon seethed with resistance activity. It was the perfect place for someone like Hall to work, dangerous enough to matter, but not so dangerous that survival was impossible.

Operating under the code name "Marie Monin," Hall began building what would become one of the most effective resistance networks in France. She started small, making contacts with local shopkeepers, farmers, and railway workers who were willing to help Allied airmen escape Nazi capture. She coordinated safe houses where downed pilots could hide while waiting for transport back to England. She organized supply drops of weapons and equipment for local resistance fighters.

Most importantly, she became the central coordinator for a web of resistance cells that stretched across central France. When resistance fighters in one area needed weapons, Hall found them. When Allied intelligence needed information about German troop movements, Hall's network provided it. When refugees needed help escaping Nazi persecution, Hall arranged safe passage.

Her wooden leg, far from being a liability, became part of her legend. She walked everywhere, sometimes twenty miles in a single day, visiting contacts, coordinating operations, and gathering intelligence. Seeing this determined American woman limping through their streets on obvious business she couldn't discuss, local French people began calling her "La Dame Qui Boite", the Lady Who Limps.

The Germans had a different name for her: "The Limping Lady." And they were desperate to catch her.

Hall's network was remarkably successful, which made it remarkably dangerous. By early 1942, the Germans knew that someone in Lyon was coordinating major resistance activities, but they couldn't figure out who. Hall's cover as an American journalist was perfect; she had legitimate reasons to move around the country, to meet with various contacts, and to ask probing questions about German activities.

But perfect covers don't last forever, especially when the enemy becomes desperate.

THE GESTAPO CLOSES IN

Figure 12: Feared by the Gestapo, known only as the Limping Lady

By late 1942, the Gestapo had identified Hall as a major security threat. Klaus Barbie, the notorious "Butcher of Lyon," made capturing her a top priority. German counterintelligence officers studying her activities were amazed by the scope and effectiveness of her network. In their reports, they described her as "the most dangerous of all Allied spies" and authorized unprecedented resources for her capture.

The net was closing. Several of Hall's key contacts had been arrested and tortured. Under extreme duress, some had revealed details about the network's operations. The Germans didn't yet know Hall's real identity, but they were getting closer. Every day she remained in Lyon increased the risk not just to herself, but to the dozens of resistance fighters who depended on her.

Hall knew she had to escape, but escape presented its own problems. The Germans controlled all major transportation routes. The Spanish border was heavily guarded. And even if she could reach Spain, there was no guarantee the supposedly neutral Spanish government wouldn't hand her over to the Gestapo.

Her only option was the most dangerous one: a winter crossing of the Pyrenees mountains on foot.

The Pyrenees in winter were a death trap. The mountain passes were buried under snow and ice. Temperatures dropped well below freezing. Even experienced mountaineers with proper equipment often died attempting winter crossings. Hall would be traveling with a small group of resistance fighters, carrying minimal supplies, using routes that existed more in hope than reality.

And she would be doing it on one good leg and one wooden one.

Figure 13: She crossed these frozen giants on foot—one step ahead of the Gestapo

THE ESCAPE THAT BECAME LEGEND

The crossing began on a November night in 1942. Hall and three French resistance fighters left Lyon by train, traveled as far south as they dared, then began walking toward the Spanish border. Their guide was a local smuggler who knew the mountain paths but warned them that winter conditions made success unlikely.

For three days, they climbed through snow and ice that cut through their inadequate clothing and froze their water supplies. Hall's wooden leg, already a challenge on flat ground, became a constant source of agony on steep mountain trails. The prosthetic rubbed raw against her stump, creating wounds that bled into her sock and froze solid overnight.

On the second night, when they stopped to rest in a cave, one of her companions suggested she couldn't continue. Hall's response, recorded later by the resistance fighter who survived to tell the story, was typical: "Cuthbert is giving me trouble, but we can handle it."

"Cuthbert" was Hall's pet name for her wooden leg. Even while fleeing for her life across one of Europe's most dangerous mountain ranges, she maintained the dry sense of humor that had carried her through two years of espionage work.

On the third day, they reached the Spanish border. Hall was exhausted, frostbitten, and barely able to walk. But she was alive, and she was free. Despite their official neutrality, the Spanish authorities allowed her to contact the British embassy. Within a week, she was back in London, debriefing SOE officers about her network's activities and planning her next mission.

Most people would have considered surviving that escape a career-ending triumph. Virginia Hall considered it a temporary setback.

RETURN TO THE FIRE

Figure 14: Seasoned by war, unshaken by fear—Hall prepared to vanish into France once more.

Hall spent six months in London, recovering from her ordeal and helping SOE analyze intelligence from her French networks. The Germans had captured many of her contacts after her escape, but the organizational structure she had built continued operating. New resistance fighters stepped in to replace those who had been arrested. The weapons and equipment she had coordinated continued to flow to French patriots fighting the occupation.

Her superiors urged her to take a desk job. She had done more than enough, they argued. She had proven that American women could operate effectively as spies. She had built networks that were saving Allied lives and disrupting German operations. She had earned the right to sit out the rest of the war in safety.

Hall disagreed. In March 1944, she transferred from British SOE to the American Office of Strategic Services (OSS), the predecessor of the CIA, and volunteered for another mission to occupied France. This time, she would go in ahead of the D-Day invasion, helping coordinate resistance activities that would support the Allied landing.

Her OSS handlers were even more worried about her safety than the British had been. The Germans now knew her face, her methods, and her capabilities. They had distributed her photograph to Gestapo offices across Europe. Returning to France would be suicidal.

Hall had a brilliant and obvious solution: she would return as someone completely different.

Figure 15: From diplomat's desk to village shadows—her greatest disguise was becoming invisible

THE MASTER OF DISGUISE

The woman who parachuted into central France in March 1944 bore little resemblance to the sophisticated American journalist who had fled across the Pyrenees. Virginia Hall had transformed herself into Marcelle Montagne, an elderly French peasant woman. She had grayed her hair, changed her posture, and adopted the slow, careful walk of someone much older than her thirty-eight years.

The transformation was so complete that even French resistance fighters who had worked with her before didn't recognize her. The Germans, searching for a tall, striking American woman with a noticeable limp, looked right past the bent old lady who tended goats in the hills of central France.

But "Marcelle Montagne" was anything but harmless. Working with a new network of resistance fighters, Hall coordinated sabotage operations that crippled German supply lines in the weeks leading up to D-Day. Her teams destroyed bridges, derailed trains, and cut communication lines that would have allowed German reinforcements to reach the Normandy beaches.

She radioed intelligence about German troop movements to Allied commanders preparing for the invasion. She coordinated supply drops that armed local resistance fighters for the battles that would follow the landing. She organized escape routes for Allied commandos operating behind enemy lines.

Most dramatically, she personally led attacks on German installations that her network had identified as high-value targets. The elderly French peasant woman could be seen limping through the countryside at night, carrying weapons and explosives to resistance fighters who would use them to harass German occupiers.

The Gestapo never figured out that their most wanted spy was hiding in plain sight, disguised as someone they would never suspect.

LIBERATION AND RECOGNITION

Figure 16: The troops marched on, unaware that the quiet old woman among the crowd had helped make their victory possible

When Allied forces broke out of the Normandy beachhead and began liberating France in the summer of 1944, Virginia Hall's networks played crucial roles in the campaign. Her resistance fighters harassed German retreats, protected Allied supply lines, and provided intelligence that helped American and British commanders avoid German counterattacks.

By August 1944, Hall was openly coordinating with advancing American forces, no longer needing to maintain her cover as a French peasant. The war in France was nearly over, and she had survived four years of World War II's most dangerous espionage work.

Her accomplishments were staggering. She had organized resistance networks that saved hundreds of Allied lives, coordinated sabotage operations that disrupted German military activities, and gathered intelligence that influenced major strategic decisions. She had escaped from Nazi-occupied territory when capture seemed certain, then returned to continue the fight under even more dangerous conditions.

In September 1945, President Harry Truman awarded Virginia Hall the Distinguished Service Cross, the only civilian woman to receive America's second-highest military decoration during World War II. The citation praised her "extraordinary heroism" and noted that her activities had "contributed materially to the success of Allied operations in France."

But the ceremony revealed something telling about how America viewed its female heroes. The presentation was held in private, with no press coverage or public recognition. Hall had requested the secrecy; she was joining the newly formed CIA and needed to maintain her anonymity, but the lack of fanfare also reflected the country's discomfort with celebrating women who had operated outside traditional gender roles.

Virginia Hall had risked everything to serve her country, but America wasn't quite ready to acknowledge that women could be warriors.

THE QUIET RETIREMENT OF A LEGEND

Figure 17; After changing the course of a war, she chose a quiet life behind a white door

After the war, Virginia Hall returned to Washington and began what would appear to be an ordinary life. She married Paul Goillot, a French OSS officer she had worked with during the war. They bought a house in suburban Maryland. She took a desk job with the CIA's analytical division, reviewing intelligence reports and briefing government officials on European affairs.

To her neighbors, Virginia Hall Goillot was a quiet, somewhat mysterious woman who had worked for the government during the war and now lived a peaceful retirement. They knew she walked with a slight limp and that she and her husband spoke French at home, but nothing more. The woman who had been the Gestapo's most wanted spy became Maryland's most anonymous suburban housewife.

Hall maintained her silence about her wartime activities for decades. The CIA kept her missions classified, and she honored that classification even after retiring. When historians occasionally contacted her about resistance activities in wartime France, she politely declined to be interviewed. When the French government wanted to award her medals for her service to the resistance, she accepted them quietly, without publicity.

It wasn't until the 1980s, when CIA files began to be declassified and French resistance records became available to researchers, that the full scope of Virginia Hall's accomplishments became clear. Even then, many details remained classified. The complete story of her wartime activities may never be fully known.

THE LEGACY OF THE LIMPING LADY

Figure 18: Once hunted in silence, now honored in bronze—Virginia Hall lives in the legacy of the CIA

Virginia Hall died in 1982, still largely unknown to the American public. The woman who had terrorized the Gestapo, organized some of the most effective resistance networks in occupied Europe, and received America's highest military honors lived her final years in suburban obscurity.

But obscurity doesn't diminish accomplishment. What Virginia Hall achieved during World War II established a template for American espionage that still influences intelligence operations. Her success proved that effective spies succeed through intelligence, preparation, and courage rather than physical intimidation or masculine bravado.

More importantly, her story challenges fundamental assumptions about heroism and capability. The State Department rejected her because they assumed her disability made her unsuitable for the foreign service. The Germans underestimated her because they couldn't imagine that a limping American woman could coordinate major resistance activities. Even her own government kept her achievements secret, partly because they weren't sure how to celebrate a female warrior.

All of them were wrong. Virginia Hall succeeded not despite her limitations, but because she refused to let other people's assumptions about her limitations become her reality. She turned her wooden leg from a liability into an asset, her outsider status from a weakness into a strength, her invisibility from a disadvantage into her greatest weapon.

In the CIA headquarters today, there is an award named in Virginia Hall's honor, given annually to officers who demonstrate exceptional courage in service to their country. The inscription notes that she "exemplified the courage, sacrifice, and dedication that define the CIA's mission."

But Hall's real legacy extends beyond the intelligence community. She proved that heroism comes in forms that challenge our expectations, that courage can be quiet as well as loud, and that the most effective warriors are often the ones no one sees coming.

The State Department official who rejected her application in 1931 probably never learned that his decision had inadvertently created one of America's greatest spies. Virginia Hall's revenge was living well enough to make his judgment look foolish.

And terrifying the Third Reich along the way.

Figure 19: A medal of valor, awarded in whispers to the woman who roared in silence

Virginia Hall's story continues to inspire intelligence officers, military personnel, and ordinary citizens who face their own seemingly impossible challenges. In an age when we often assume that heroes must be perfect people making perfect decisions, she reminds us that real heroism comes from imperfect people refusing to accept imperfect circumstances. Sometimes the most patriotic thing you can do is prove your country wrong about what you're capable of achieving.

Chapter 2:
America's Secret Army Wore Lipstick

THE WOMEN WHO CRACKED CODES AND CHANGED HISTORY

Figure 20: Behind closed doors, they unraveled secrets that shaped the fate of nations

The help-wanted ad appeared in newspapers across America in early 1942, buried between advertisements for Victory Garden seeds and requests for scrap metal donations. "Wanted: Women with college degrees for essential war work in Washington. Mathematics, language, or science background preferred. Immediate start. High security clearance required."

What the ad didn't mention was that the women who answered it would become America's most secret weapon, a hidden army of codebreakers, analysts, and intelligence operatives who would help win World War II from behind desks in anonymous government buildings. While their brothers and boyfriends fought with rifles and tanks, these women waged war with pencils and slide rules, turning intercepted enemy messages into Allied victories.

They called themselves "government girls," but they were really America's first large-scale deployment of female intelligence officers. And like Virginia Hall, their stories were classified for decades after the war ended.

The difference was that Hall worked alone. These women worked in teams of hundreds, creating an intelligence apparatus that would reshape how America gathered and analyzed information about its enemies. Their success would lay the foundation for the CIA, the NSA, and the modern American intelligence community.

But in 1942, they were just young women looking for meaningful work in wartime Washington, with no idea they were about to become secret warriors.

THE MATHEMATICS OF WAR

Figure 21: Grace Hopper: coding a new world where logic meets legacy

Dorothy Blum arrived in Washington, D.C. in March 1942 with a mathematics degree from the University of Pennsylvania and no clear idea what her new job would involve. The Navy recruiter who had interviewed her on campus had been vague about details, mentioning only that her mathematical skills were needed for "important war work" that would require absolute secrecy.

Blum discovered a revolution in the making when she reported to the Navy's Communications Security Section. The U.S. military was racing to crack Japanese and German codes that could reveal enemy battle plans, troop movements, and strategic intentions. Success would save American lives and shorten the war. Failure could mean losing the war entirely.

The problem was that breaking sophisticated enemy codes required mathematical skills that few military officers possessed. The traditional military approach, throwing more manpower at the problem, wouldn't work when the problem required advanced mathematics, language skills, and analytical thinking rather than physical strength or combat experience.

The solution was radical for 1942: recruit the most mathematically gifted college graduates in America, regardless of gender, and teach them to be codebreakers.

The result was an intelligence workforce that was more than 70% female, a percentage that would be remarkable even today, and was revolutionary in the 1940s. In their early twenties, most of these women became America's secret mathematical army.

Blum's first assignment was analyzing Japanese diplomatic codes. Every day, Navy interceptors would capture dozens of encrypted Japanese messages sent between Tokyo and Japanese embassies worldwide. The messages arrived as seemingly random sequences of numbers that made no obvious sense: "47391 85027 63948 21756…"

Blum's job was to find patterns in those numbers that would reveal the underlying message. It required mathematical intuition, linguistic analysis, and detective work that could take hours or days for a single message. Most importantly, it required the kind of analytical thinking that couldn't be rushed or forced; the enemy had to be outsmarted, not overpowered.

The work was mentally exhausting and often frustrating. Blum and her colleagues would spend days analyzing a message, certain they had found the key to breaking it, only to discover that their solution produced gibberish. Then they would start over, looking for different patterns, testing new theories, hoping that the next approach would unlock enemy secrets.

But when it worked, the results were spectacular. A successfully decoded Japanese message might reveal that the enemy was planning an attack on a specific Allied position, allowing American commanders to prepare defenses or launch preemptive strikes. A broken German code could expose U-boat patrol routes, enabling Allied convoys to avoid submarine attacks that would have sunk ships and killed sailors.

Dorothy Blum and her colleagues weren't just solving mathematical puzzles. They were saving lives with slide rules and statistical analysis.

THE SECRET SISTERHOOD

Figure 22: They cracked codes, not glass ceilings—together, they shaped the silence of victory

As more women arrived in Washington to work in the rapidly expanding intelligence apparatus, they formed a unique community. Living in overcrowded boarding houses and government dormitories, working twelve-hour shifts in windowless offices, sworn to secrecy about their jobs, they created their own social networks and support systems.

Ruth Weston, who joined the Army Signal Intelligence Service in 1943, later described the atmosphere: "We were all young women, mostly away from home for the first time, doing work we couldn't discuss with anyone outside our group. We became each other's families."

The secrecy requirements created both isolation and intimacy. The women couldn't tell their families, friends, or boyfriends what they did for work. When people asked, they would say they were "filing papers" or "doing clerical work for the government." The vague descriptions reinforced stereotypes about women's wartime roles while hiding the sophisticated analytical work they actually performed.

But within their secure facilities, they could discuss the intellectual challenges and emotional pressures of their jobs. They celebrated together when they cracked a particularly difficult code. They supported each other through the frustration of failing to break messages that might contain crucial intelligence. They shared the satisfaction of knowing that their work was making a real difference in the war effort.

Figure 23: They listened as the world changed—knowing they had quietly helped change it.

Ann Mitchell, who worked on German codes for the Office of Strategic Services, remembered the weight of responsibility that came with their secret knowledge: "Sometimes we would decode messages about planned attacks or troop movements, and then we would hear on the radio news about battles in those exact locations. We knew our work had contributed to saving American lives, but we couldn't tell anyone. It was simultaneously the most meaningful and most isolating experience of our lives."

The women developed their own internal culture and terminology. They called particularly difficult codes "stubborn Germans" or "tricky Japs" (using language that was acceptable in the 1940s but would be inappropriate today). They nicknamed their most sophisticated cipher machines and developed shorthand methods for communicating about their work without revealing classified information.

Most importantly, they developed an esprit de corps that sustained them through the mental exhaustion and emotional pressure of their jobs. They were part of something larger than themselves, and they knew their contribution was essential to the war effort, even if the world would never acknowledge their achievements.

BREAKING THE UNBREAKABLE

Figure 24: A machine of secrets—decoded by minds sharper than its gears.

The most spectacular success of America's female codebreakers came in 1940, two years before most of them had even been recruited. The target was Japan's most sophisticated diplomatic cipher, code-named "Purple" by American intelligence. The Japanese considered Purple unbreakable, and for good reason.

Purple used an electromechanical cipher machine that created encrypted messages through a series of electrical switches and rotors. The machine had millions of possible settings, and the Japanese changed those settings regularly. Breaking Purple required not just mathematical analysis, but reverse-engineering an incredibly complex piece of technology that American codebreakers had never seen.

The team assigned to crack Purple was led by William Friedman, one of America's greatest cryptanalysts. Still, much of the actual analytical work was performed by women mathematicians who had been recruited specifically for their problem-solving abilities. Genevieve Grotjan, a mathematics graduate from the University of Buffalo, made the crucial breakthrough that revealed Purple's underlying logical structure.

Figure 25: In the hum of silence, her insight cracked the uncrackable.

Working eighteen-hour days for months, Grotjan analyzed thousands of Purple messages, looking for patterns that would reveal how the cipher machine operated. The work was like trying to reverse-engineer a watch by studying the time it displayed, without ever seeing the internal mechanism.

In September 1940, Grotjan noticed a subtle pattern in the way certain letters appeared in encrypted messages. The pattern was so slight that it could easily be missed, but it suggested that Purple's cipher machine had a logical vulnerability that could be exploited. Working with her colleagues, she developed a mathematical attack that successfully predicted how Purple would encrypt new messages.

The breakthrough was stunning. American codebreakers could now read Japan's most secret diplomatic communications in real time, often before the intended recipients received them. This intelligence windfall, code-named "Magic" by American officials, provided advance warning of Japanese intentions and strategies throughout the war.

Magic intelligence revealed Japanese plans for attacking Pearl Harbor, though the warnings were too vague and arrived too late to prevent the attack. It provided detailed information about Japanese military preparations for major battles across the Pacific. Most crucially, it allowed American commanders to anticipate Japanese strategies and position their forces accordingly.

Genevieve Grotjan's mathematical breakthrough had given America the ability to read the enemy's mind. But her achievement remained classified for thirty years after the war ended, and she received no public recognition during her lifetime.

THE PROPAGANDA WARRIORS

Figure 26: With ink and insight, she fought a war of minds across oceans

While most female intelligence operatives worked with codes and ciphers, others fought a different kind of secret war: the battle for hearts and minds. Betty McIntosh joined the Office of Strategic Services in 1943 and was assigned to create propaganda designed to demoralize Japanese soldiers and civilians.

McIntosh's job was to get inside the enemy's head and figure out what messages would be most psychologically devastating. Working from OSS offices in India and China, she created fake Japanese newspapers filled with stories about American military successes and Japanese defeats. She wrote radio scripts designed to make Japanese soldiers homesick and demoralized. She developed leaflets that could be dropped over Japanese positions to encourage surrender or desertion.

The work required a deep understanding of Japanese culture, psychology, and current events. McIntosh had to think like a Japanese soldier or civilian while remaining completely loyal to the American war effort. She had to create lies that were convincing enough to fool native Japanese speakers, while embedding those lies in enough truth to make them believable.

Figure 27: With paper and persuasion, she planted doubt behind enemy lines

Her most successful operation involved creating a fictitious Japanese general who supposedly had been captured by American forces and was now encouraging Japanese soldiers to surrender. McIntosh wrote speeches for this non-existent general, recorded them using a Japanese-American actor, and broadcast them over radio frequencies that Japanese troops were known to monitor.

The fake general's surrender appeals were so convincing that Japanese military commanders issued specific orders warning their troops not to listen to his broadcasts. American intelligence intercepted those orders, proving that McIntosh's psychological warfare campaign was having its intended effect.

But propaganda work took an emotional toll that was different from codebreaking. McIntosh was creating materials designed to break enemy morale and encourage surrender. She was trying to convince young Japanese soldiers that their cause was hopeless, their leaders had abandoned them, and their best option was to give up fighting.

"I was trying to save lives on both sides," McIntosh later explained. "Every Japanese soldier who surrendered because of something I wrote was one less person who would die in a battle that Japan couldn't win anyway. But spending my days trying to destroy other people's hope was still emotionally difficult."

THE DOUBLE LIFE

Figure 28: Just another face on the street—carrying the weight of a nation's secrets

The secrecy requirements of intelligence work created a peculiar kind of double life for the women who performed it. During the day, they were analyzing enemy communications, breaking sophisticated codes, and creating psychological warfare materials that could influence major military operations. In the evenings, they returned to boarding houses and social events where they had to pretend they spent their days filing papers and answering phones.

Virginia Aderholdt, who worked on German codes for the Army Signal Intelligence Service, described the psychological challenge: "I would spend ten hours breaking codes that revealed German battle plans for major offensives on the Russian front. Then I would go to dinner with friends who would ask what I did at work, and I would have to say I couldn't talk about it because it was 'boring clerical stuff.' The disconnect was surreal."

The women developed elaborate strategies for deflecting questions about their work. They would change the subject, claim they were too tired to discuss their jobs, or give vague answers about "government paperwork" that discouraged further inquiry. Some created entirely fictitious job descriptions that sounded plausible but revealed nothing about their actual responsibilities.

Figure 29: Laughter by night, secrets by day—every gathering a perfect cover.

The secrecy was particularly difficult when it came to romantic relationships. Many of the women were dating military officers who were fighting overseas or preparing for combat assignments. Their boyfriends would write letters describing their military experiences, but the women couldn't reciprocate with details about their own contributions to the war effort.

Some relationships ended because of the secrecy requirements. Men who were risking their lives in combat couldn't understand why their girlfriends wouldn't discuss their "safe" jobs in Washington. The women couldn't explain that their work was actually more sensitive than most military assignments, requiring security clearances that many combat officers didn't have.

Others found ways to navigate the complications. Dorothy Blum married a Navy officer who also worked in intelligence, which meant they could discuss at least some aspects of their jobs with each other. Ruth Weston dated a civilian engineer who understood that wartime work often involved classified projects and didn't pressure her for details about her assignments.

But for most of the women, the war years involved a constant tension between their significant professional accomplishments and their inability to share those accomplishments with the people closest to them.

THE END OF THE WAR, THE BEGINNING OF SILENCE

Figure 30: With victory came silence—filing away heroism, one folder at a time

When Japan surrendered in August 1945, America's female intelligence operatives faced an uncertain future. The massive wartime intelligence apparatus was being dismantled. Many of the women who had spent three or four years breaking enemy codes and analyzing intelligence were told their services were no longer needed.

The official message was clear: the emergency that had required women to perform sophisticated analytical work was over. America was returning to normal, which meant that women would return to traditional roles as wives, mothers, and clerical workers.

Some of the women did exactly that. They married, moved to the suburbs, and spent the rest of their lives keeping their wartime accomplishments secret from their children and grandchildren. They had helped win the greatest war in human history, but couldn't talk about it at PTA meetings or neighborhood coffee gatherings.

Others fought to continue their intelligence careers. Dorothy Blum stayed with the Navy's cryptanalysis program, eventually becoming one of the first female supervisors in the newly formed National Security

Agency. Genevieve Grotjan continued working on code-breaking projects for the Army Security Agency. Betty McIntosh joined the Central Intelligence Agency when it was created in 1947.

But even the women who continued working in intelligence found that their wartime achievements were being written out of the official record. Histories of World War II codebreaking focused on male leaders like William Friedman while barely mentioning the women who had performed much of the actual analytical work.

The women themselves were complicit in this historical erasure, but they had little choice. Their work remained classified, and they had sworn oaths of secrecy that they took seriously. When historians or journalists asked about wartime intelligence operations, the women would deflect questions or claim they didn't remember details about classified work.

Some found indirect ways to acknowledge their contributions. Ruth Weston became a mathematics teacher and would tell her students that "women played important roles in World War II that most people don't know about." Dorothy Blum mentored young women entering government service, encouraging them to pursue careers in technical fields that had traditionally excluded women.

But for the most part, America's secret army of female intelligence operatives simply faded back into civilian anonymity, carrying their achievements like buried treasure that couldn't be shared with anyone.

THE SECRET THAT SHAPED THE FUTURE

Figure 31: From hidden rooms to modern towers—the legacy of quiet brilliance endures

The declassification of World War II intelligence records in the 1970s and 1980s finally revealed the scope of women's contributions to Allied victory. Historians studying newly released documents were amazed to discover that women had performed much of the analytical work that broke enemy codes, provided crucial intelligence, and shaped major strategic decisions.

The revelation transformed understanding of both women's capabilities and the nature of modern warfare. The women who had been dismissed as "filing clerks" and "government girls" were revealed to have been America's first generation of professional intelligence analysts.

More importantly, their success established precedents that would influence American intelligence operations for decades. The CIA, NSA, and other agencies created after the war continued recruiting women for analytical positions, building on the wartime discovery that gender was irrelevant to intelligence work.

Many of the techniques developed by female codebreakers during World War II became standard practices in the intelligence community. The mathematical approaches pioneered by women like Genevieve Grotjan influenced the development of computer-based code-breaking systems. The psychological warfare methods created by women like Betty McIntosh became templates for Cold War propaganda operations.

Figure 32 From paper codes to digital frontlines—her vigilance is the modern legacy of wartime pioneers.

But perhaps most significantly, the women's wartime achievements proved that effective intelligence work required intellectual capabilities rather than physical strength or masculine aggression. Their success helped redefine what kinds of people could serve as intelligence officers and what methods were most effective for gathering and analyzing information about America's enemies.

Today, women make up nearly 50% of the CIA's workforce and hold senior positions throughout the intelligence community. The director of the CIA has been a woman, as have the directors of major NSA divisions and other intelligence agencies. This level of female participation in intelligence work traces directly back to the wartime precedent established by the "government girls" of World War II.

THE UNFINISHED RECOGNITION

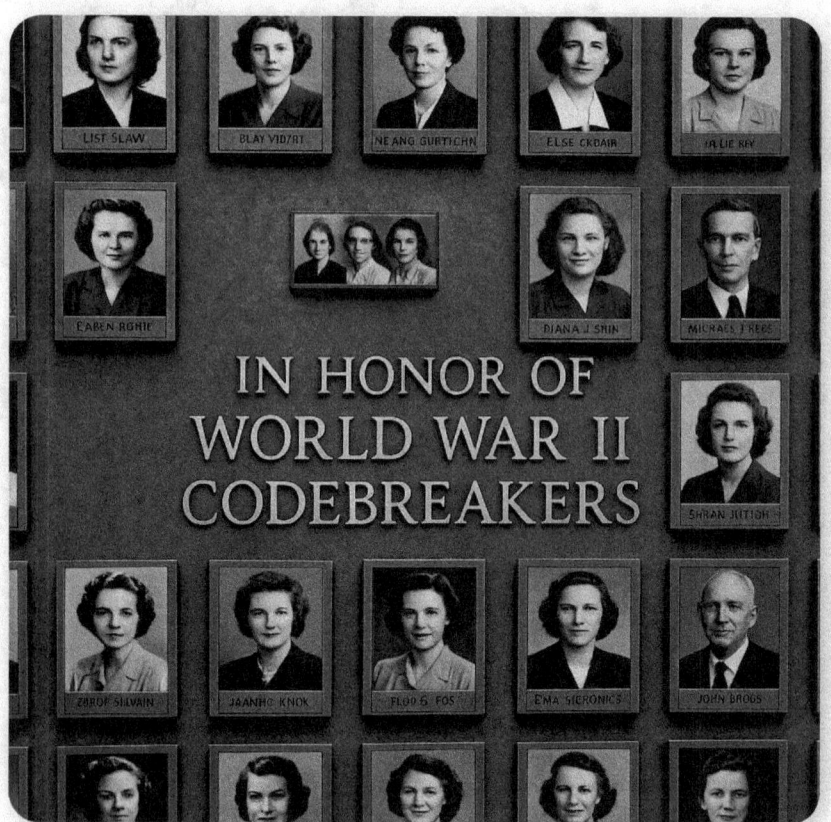

Figure 33: Their names etched in stone—once hidden, now honored for decoding history.

In 2019, the National Security Agency finally created a memorial honoring the World War II codebreakers who had helped establish American signals intelligence capabilities. The memorial includes individual plaques for key personnel, and visitors can see that a remarkable number of the honored codebreakers were women.

But full recognition has been slow in coming. Many of the women who performed crucial intelligence work during World War II died before their achievements became public knowledge. Their families often learned about their wartime accomplishments only after reading declassified documents or historical accounts published decades after the war ended.

Dorothy Blum lived to see some recognition of her contributions, receiving awards from the Navy and NSA for her codebreaking work. But she was in her eighties before she could publicly discuss what she had accomplished as a young mathematician in wartime Washington.

Genevieve Grotjan never received significant public recognition for her breakthrough on the Purple cipher. She died in 2006, still largely unknown outside the intelligence community despite making one of American history's most important cryptanalytic discoveries.

Betty McIntosh wrote memoirs about her OSS experiences, but they weren't published until she was in her nineties. By then, most Americans had forgotten that psychological warfare had been a crucial component of the Allied victory, and that much of that work had been performed by young women operating behind enemy lines.

Figure 34: Decades later, she holds the proof of a war quietly won.

The delayed recognition reflects broader patterns in how America remembers its wartime heroes. Combat veterans receive immediate and ongoing recognition for their service. Intelligence operatives, especially female intelligence operatives, must wait decades for their achievements to be acknowledged.

But the delay doesn't diminish the achievement. The women who cracked enemy codes, analyzed intelligence, and waged psychological warfare during World War II proved that heroism comes in many forms. They demonstrated that wars are won not just by soldiers with weapons, but by analysts with slide rules, linguists with dictionaries, and mathematicians with stubborn determination to solve impossible puzzles.

Their secret army wore lipstick instead of combat boots, but they were warriors nonetheless. And their victories helped save the world.

The legacy of America's female intelligence operatives during World War II continues to influence how the country approaches national security challenges. Their success proved that effective intelligence work requires diversity of thought, analytical sophistication, and the kind of intellectual courage that refuses to accept defeat. In an era when America faces new and complex security threats, the example of the "government girls" reminds us that our greatest weapons are often carried in briefcases rather than holsters, and that our most effective warriors often work in offices rather than on battlefields.

Chapter 3:
The Price of Victory

WHAT IT COST THE WOMEN WHO SAVED THE WORLD

Figure 35: The world cheered, but she sat in silence—her victory sworn to secrecy

𝕿he nightmares started six months after the war ended.

Sarah Chen had spent three years analyzing Japanese military codes for the Army Signal Intelligence Service, working twelve-hour shifts in a windowless basement office in Arlington. She had decoded messages that revealed enemy attack plans, intercepted communications that saved Allied lives, and helped break cipher systems that the Japanese military considered unbreakable.

But now, in the spring of 1946, she would wake up at three in the morning with her heart racing, convinced that Japanese agents were following her. She would check the locks on her apartment door multiple times before going to bed. She would flinch when strangers spoke to her in foreign languages on Washington's crowded streetcars.

The war was over. America had won. And Sarah Chen was falling apart.

She wasn't alone. Across the country, women who had served as America's secret intelligence operatives were struggling with psychological wounds that had no name and no treatment. They had lived for years under constant stress, carrying secrets that could get them killed, analyzing enemy communications that revealed the full horror of global warfare. Now they were expected to return to normal civilian lives as if nothing had happened.

But they had seen too much, known too much, and carried too much to ever be normal again.

Figure 36: In a room of silence, the mind's scars went unseen and unnamed

THE WEIGHT OF SECRETS

The psychological burden of intelligence work during World War II was unlike anything previous generations of American women had experienced. Unlike combat soldiers, who could share their experiences with fellow veterans and receive recognition for their service, intelligence operatives were sworn to lifelong secrecy about their contributions to the war effort.

They couldn't tell their families what they had done. They couldn't seek therapy for work-related stress without risking their security clearances. They couldn't even commiserate with former colleagues, since discussing classified work outside secure facilities was forbidden regardless of the war's outcome.

Most importantly, they couldn't receive the social recognition and collective healing that helped other veterans transition back to civilian life. While combat veterans were celebrated as heroes and supported by new programs like the GI Bill, intelligence operatives were expected to disappear back into anonymous civilian lives without acknowledgment or assistance.

Figure 37: They stood in silence as the parade passed—veterans without uniforms, medals, or recognition.

Dorothy Blum, the Navy mathematician who had spent the war breaking Japanese codes, later described the psychological isolation: "We had been part of something enormous and important, something that helped save millions of lives and win the war. But we couldn't talk about it with anyone. We couldn't even talk about it with each other once we left the secure facilities. It was like our entire wartime experience had been erased from our own lives."

The secrecy requirements meant that many of the women couldn't explain to their families why they sometimes seemed distant or troubled. Parents and siblings who had worried about their daughters and sisters working in "dangerous" Washington during the war couldn't understand why these women seemed more stressed after the war ended than they had during the fighting.

Romantic relationships were particularly challenging. Many of the women had postponed marriage during the war, focusing on their intelligence work while their boyfriends served overseas. When the men returned from combat, they expected to resume normal relationships with women who seemed fundamentally changed by experiences they couldn't discuss.

Veterans Administration hospitals in the late 1940s began seeing a puzzling phenomenon: young women seeking treatment for anxiety, insomnia, and depression, but unable to explain what had caused their symptoms. The women would describe vague "government work" during the war, but couldn't provide details that would help doctors understand their psychological distress.

The medical profession in the 1940s had limited understanding of what would later be called post-traumatic stress disorder, and virtually no understanding of how psychological trauma might affect civilians who had been exposed to the stress of war without actually experiencing combat. The women's symptoms were often dismissed as "female hysteria" or "adjustment problems" that would resolve themselves once the women settled into proper domestic roles.

THE BURDEN OF KNOWLEDGE

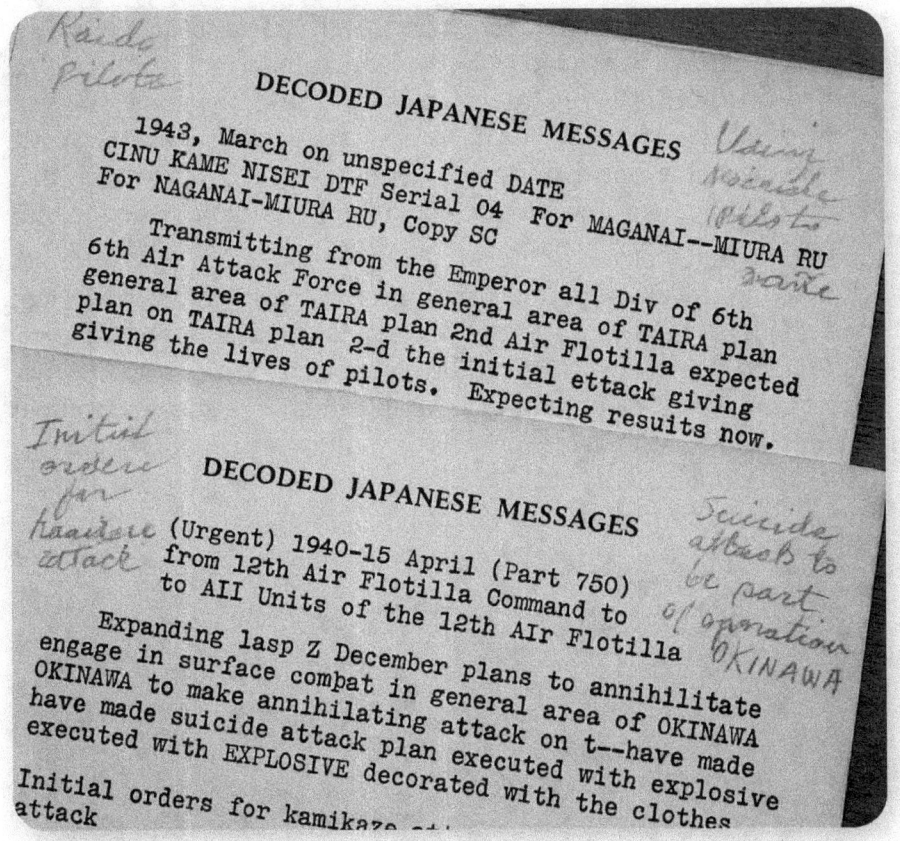

Figure 38: Each decoded word revealed a nightmare—read, translated, and carried in silence

Beyond the secrecy requirements, the women who had worked in intelligence carried a psychological burden that was uniquely devastating: they knew too much about human cruelty and the machinery of war.

Combat soldiers experienced the immediate horror of battle, but their exposure was typically limited to specific engagements and geographical areas. Intelligence operatives, by contrast, had a comprehensive view of the entire war's brutality. They read intercepted messages describing mass executions, analyzed reports of systematic starvation and torture, and decoded communications that revealed the full scope of Nazi genocide and Japanese war crimes.

Ann Mitchell, who had worked on German codes for the OSS, later described the cumulative psychological impact: "Every day, we would decode messages that described atrocities that were almost impossible to believe. We knew about the Holocaust before most Americans learned it existed. We read German communications about the systematic murder of civilians, the deliberate starvation of prisoners, and the medical experiments on children. And we had to process that information analytically, without letting our emotional reactions interfere with our work."

The women were expected to maintain professional detachment while analyzing communications that revealed humanity at its worst. They had to transform horrific information into sanitized intelligence reports that could be used by military commanders and government officials. The emotional cost of this constant exposure to documented atrocity was enormous, but there was no recognition that such work might require psychological support.

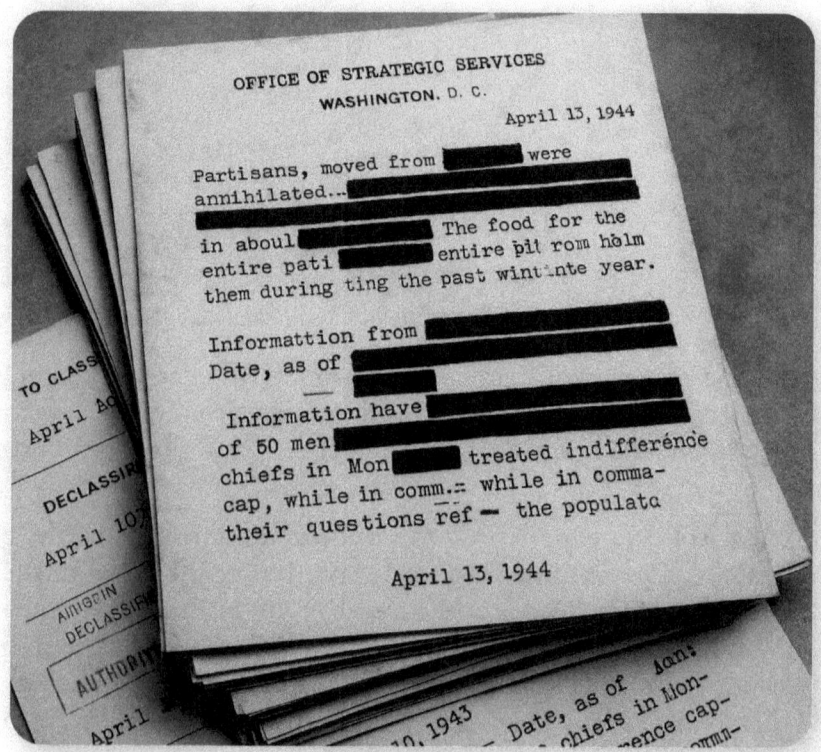

Figure 39: At the bottom of every blacked-out line was a truth too brutal to say aloud

Betty McIntosh, who had created psychological warfare materials for the OSS, faced a different but equally troubling psychological challenge. Her job required her to understand enemy psychology well enough to create propaganda that would demoralize Japanese soldiers and civilians. This meant spending her days thinking about the most effective ways to destroy other people's hope and will to fight.

"I became very good at understanding what would break someone's spirit," McIntosh later wrote. "I knew exactly which messages would make a Japanese soldier homesick enough to consider desertion, which appeals would convince civilians that their cause was hopeless. But that knowledge was like carrying poison in my head. I understood too much about human vulnerability and couldn't forget what I had learned."

The psychological warfare specialists faced an additional burden: they weren't just analyzing enemy atrocities, they were actively participating in the war's psychological dimension. While their work was intended to shorten the war and save lives on both sides, it still required them to spend their days crafting messages designed to destroy other human beings' morale and mental resilience.

THE CYANIDE GIRLS

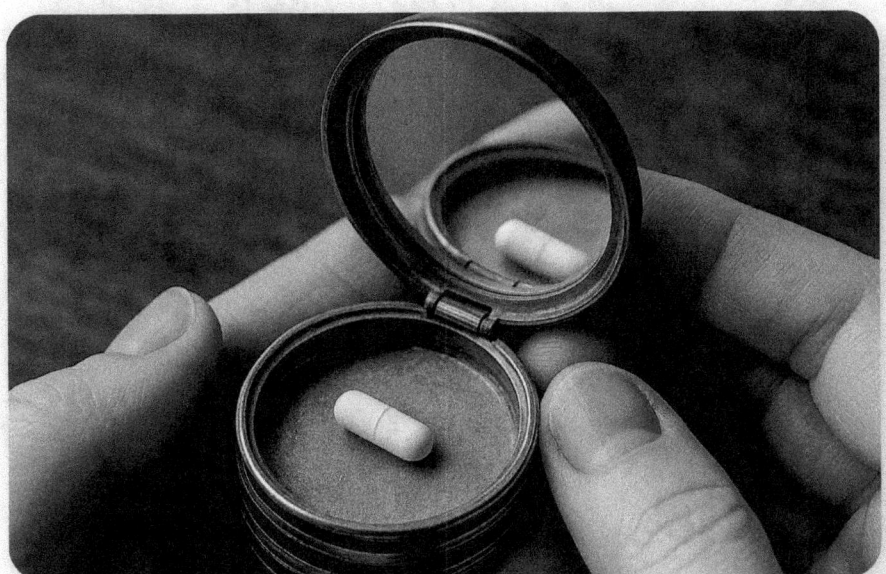

Figure 40: Disguised in elegance, it held her final act of defiance

The women who had served as field operatives faced psychological challenges that were even more severe than those experienced by the codebreakers and analysts. Virginia Hall and the other female agents who had operated behind enemy lines had lived for years under the constant threat of capture, torture, and execution.

Unlike military personnel, who were protected by the Geneva Convention's rules governing the treatment of prisoners of war, intelligence operatives who were captured could expect no mercy. The Germans and Japanese routinely tortured captured spies to extract information about resistance networks and Allied operations. Female agents were particularly vulnerable to sexual violence and humiliation designed to break their psychological resistance.

To prevent enemy interrogators from extracting crucial information, many female agents carried suicide pills, small cyanide capsules that could be bitten if capture seemed imminent. The pills were hidden in jewelry, lipstick cases, or clothing, always within easy reach if the situation became desperate.

Figure 41: *They were given chairs to heal—she was given silence to endure*

Living with constant awareness that death was literally at hand created a unique form of psychological stress. The women had to function normally while knowing that any day might require them to make a split-second decision about whether life was still worth living.

After the war, many of these women struggled with what psychologists would later recognize as survivor's guilt. They had lived through experiences that killed many of their colleagues and contacts. They had made life-or-death decisions that saved some people while dooming others. They had survived situations where survival often depended on luck as much as skill.

Ruth Norberg, who had operated radio equipment for resistance networks in Norway, later described the psychological aftermath: "During the war, I was too busy staying alive to think about the emotional impact of what I was experiencing. After the war, all of that suppressed fear and trauma came flooding back. I would have panic attacks in crowded places, convinced that everyone around me was a potential enemy. I couldn't sleep without checking escape routes from whatever room I was in. I had trained myself to be paranoid and couldn't turn that training off."

The field operatives also struggled with readjusting to a peacetime world that seemed impossibly naive about human nature and international relations. They had seen how quickly civilization could collapse, how easily ordinary people could become collaborators or executioners, how thin the line was between safety and catastrophe.

This knowledge made it difficult for them to engage in normal civilian activities or relationships. Social gatherings seemed trivial when compared to the life-or-death stakes they had navigated during the war. Domestic concerns felt insignificant when measured against the global survival issues they had helped address.

THE RETURN TO "NORMAL"

Figure 42: They served in silence—then watched the world reassign them to the kitchen.

American society in 1945 was eager to return to prewar normalcy, and that meant women returning to traditional domestic roles. The massive mobilization of women for war work was viewed as a temporary emergency measure, not a permanent change in gender relations, with the war over, cultural and economic pressure mounted for women to leave their jobs and make room for returning male veterans.

This transition was difficult but manageable for women who had performed routine industrial or clerical work during the war. For women who had served as intelligence operatives, it was psychologically devastating.

They were being asked to pretend that their wartime experiences, which had been among the most significant and meaningful work of their lives, had never happened. They were expected to find fulfillment in domestic activities after having helped coordinate military operations that affected the fate of nations. They were supposed to be satisfied with social conversations about recipes and child-rearing after having spent years analyzing enemy strategy and conducting psychological warfare.

Figure 43: Her hands scrubbed dishes, but her mind lingered on secrets she was never allowed to tell.

Virginia Aderholdt, who had worked on German codes for the Army Signal Intelligence Service, later described the psychological whiplash: "One day I was breaking codes that revealed German battle plans for major offensives. Six months later, I was expected to be thrilled about choosing wallpaper patterns for my new suburban home. The disconnect was surreal. I had been trusted with some of the most important secrets in the world, and now I was supposed to find meaning in organizing my husband's sock drawer."

Some women tried to maintain intellectual engagement by pursuing advanced education. Universities in the late 1940s saw an unusual number of applications from women seeking graduate degrees in mathematics, languages, and international relations. But these women faced new challenges: they couldn't explain their wartime experience in applications or interviews, which meant they appeared to be dilettantes rather than serious scholars with a relevant background.

Others sought careers that would utilize their analytical skills, but found that most employers were uninterested in hiring women for positions that required serious intellectual engagement. The same society that had been willing to trust women with breaking enemy codes was unwilling to trust them with managing corporate budgets or analyzing market trends.

Many of the women simply gave up and accepted traditional domestic roles, but the psychological cost was enormous. They had proven to themselves that they were capable of extraordinary intellectual and professional achievement, but society was telling them that such capabilities were no longer needed or wanted.

THE SILENT BREAKDOWN

Figure 44: Diagnosed as 'nerves,' dismissed as 'hysteria'—their silent scars had no name in the postwar home

By the early 1950s, mental health professionals were noticing a troubling pattern among young women who had worked for the government during the war. These women showed unusually high rates of anxiety, depression, and what psychiatrists of the era called "nervous exhaustion."

The women's symptoms were often severe: chronic insomnia, panic attacks, difficulty concentrating, and social withdrawal. But when doctors asked about possible causes, the women could only provide vague explanations about "stressful government work" during the war.

The medical profession's response was shaped by the limited understanding of trauma and the cultural assumptions about women's psychological fragility. Many doctors concluded that these women had been damaged by exposure to work that was "too demanding" for the female constitution. The prescribed treatment was usually rest, sedatives, and a return to purely domestic activities.

Figure 45: Labeled and dispensed—treatment wrapped in misunderstanding

This medical interpretation actually reinforced the cultural narrative that women's wartime work had been an unfortunate necessity that had harmed the women involved. It supported the argument that women should be protected from demanding professional responsibilities to preserve their mental health.

The women themselves often accepted this interpretation because they had no framework for understanding their experiences differently. The concept of post-traumatic stress disorder wouldn't be formally recognized until the 1970s, and even then, it was primarily associated with combat veterans rather than intelligence operatives.

Many of the women became convinced that they were somehow defective or weak for struggling with psychological symptoms. They internalized the shame of not being able to "adjust" to normal peacetime life, not understanding that their symptoms were normal responses to abnormal experiences.

Dorothy Blum later described this period: "I thought there was something wrong with me because I couldn't be happy doing the things other women seemed to enjoy. I didn't understand that I was grieving for a part of my life that had been enormously meaningful, but that I could never discuss or reclaim. I thought I was being ungrateful or neurotic."

THE COPING MECHANISMS

Figure 46: They traded codebooks for cookbooks—but never stopped serving their country

Despite the lack of formal support, many of the women found ways to cope with their psychological challenges and channel their skills into peacetime activities.

Some became teachers, finding that education provided intellectual engagement and social meaning without requiring them to discuss their classified background. Mathematics and language teachers who had been wartime codebreakers could use their analytical skills while maintaining their security clearances.

Others threw themselves into volunteer work, particularly activities related to international relations or veterans' affairs. They couldn't discuss their own service, but they could support other veterans and work on causes related to international understanding and conflict prevention.

A significant number became involved in early computer development, recognizing that the new electronic calculating machines represented an evolution of the analytical work they had performed during the war. Companies like IBM and Burroughs hired women with mathematical backgrounds for programming positions, not knowing that many of their employees had been among America's most sophisticated intelligence analysts.

Figure 47: From secret codes to silicon circuits—the silent pioneers of the digital age.

Some found ways to maintain connections with former colleagues, creating informal networks that provided mutual support without violating security requirements. These women would socialize together, understanding that they shared experiences they couldn't discuss but could acknowledge through meaningful glances and careful omissions in conversation.

Betty McIntosh became a writer, channeling her propaganda skills into journalism and eventually fiction. She couldn't write about her OSS experiences, but she could explore themes of international conflict, cultural misunderstanding, and the psychological impact of war through other stories.

Ruth Weston returned to graduate school and became a research mathematician, finding that academic work provided the intellectual challenge she needed while allowing her to work independently. She later said that pure mathematics felt "clean" after years of applied analytical work that had been focused on destroying enemy capabilities.

THE LONG ROAD TO RECOGNITION

Figure 48: Forty years later, the truth finally had her name on it

The psychological healing process for many of these women didn't begin until decades after the war ended, when government files began to be declassified and their contributions became part of the public record.

In the 1970s and 1980s, when historians gained access to previously classified documents about wartime intelligence operations, many former operatives learned for the first time how significant their contributions had been. They discovered that operations they had considered routine analytical work had actually influenced major strategic decisions. They realized that their individual efforts had been part of intelligence programs that had shortened the war and saved thousands of lives.

This late recognition was both healing and painful. The women felt validated in their sense that their wartime work had been extraordinarily important. Still, they also grieved for the decades they had spent believing that their contributions were somehow less significant than those of other veterans.

Figure 49: With her secrets now declassified, a family finally understands the hidden heroism of their loved one.

Sarah Chen, who had struggled with nightmares and anxiety for years after the war, finally found peace in the 1980s when she was able to attend a reunion of former Signal Intelligence Service personnel. For the first time in forty years, she could discuss her wartime experiences with people who understood what she had lived through.

"It was like being able to breathe again," she later said. "For decades, I had carried these experiences alone, wondering if I had imagined how important the work had been. When I could finally talk about it with other people who had been there, I realized that my memories were accurate and my pride was justified."

The reunions and historical recognition also revealed that many of the women had developed similar coping mechanisms and psychological strategies for dealing with their experiences. They discovered that symptoms they had thought were personal failings were actually common responses to the unique stresses of intelligence work.

THE MODERN UNDERSTANDING

Figure 50: After decades of silence, she finally tells them the truth

Modern psychology's understanding of trauma and stress provides context for the experiences of women who served in intelligence roles during World War II. Their symptoms, hypervigilance, social withdrawal, difficulty with intimate relationships, and chronic anxiety, are now recognized as normal responses to prolonged exposure to life-threatening stress and horrific information.

Contemporary therapists understand that intelligence operatives face unique psychological challenges that are different from but equally severe as those experienced by combat veterans. The constant secrecy, the exposure to detailed information about human atrocities, the responsibility for making decisions that affect other people's lives, and the social isolation that comes with classified work all create psychological pressures that can have lasting effects.

The women who served as America's intelligence operatives during World War II were pioneers not just in terms of breaking gender barriers in national security work, but also in terms of experiencing psychological challenges that the medical profession wasn't equipped to understand or treat.

Figure 51: A modern therapist's office, equipped with books on trauma and PTSD, symbolizes the understanding and support that came decades too late for many wartime intelligence veterans

Their experiences helped establish the understanding that all forms of military and intelligence service can result in psychological wounds that require professional treatment and social support. The recognition that these women deserved the same care and honor as other veterans helped expand society's definition of who counts as a veteran and what kinds of service warrant recognition and support.

THE INHERITANCE OF COURAGE

Figure 52: A modern female intelligence analyst continues the legacy of WWII's pioneering codebreakers

The women who paid the psychological price for America's intelligence victories during World War II left a complex legacy. Their sacrifices helped establish the precedent that women could serve effectively in the most sensitive national security positions. Their success proved that intellectual courage was just as important as physical bravery in defending the country.

But their experiences also revealed the importance of providing appropriate support for people who serve in high-stress, classified positions. The modern intelligence community has learned from their example, providing psychological services and peer support programs that weren't available to the World War II generation.

Today's female intelligence officers still face many of the same challenges: the secrecy requirements, the exposure to disturbing information, and the social isolation that comes with classified work. But they also benefit from institutional recognition that such work carries psychological costs that require professional attention.

The women who broke codes, analyzed intelligence, and conducted psychological warfare during World War II proved that heroism often comes with a price that isn't immediately visible. They demonstrated that serving your country sometimes means carrying burdens that can't be shared, processing experiences that can't be discussed, and finding ways to heal from wounds that society doesn't recognize.

Their courage wasn't just in the dangerous work they performed during the war. It was also in the quiet strength they showed in rebuilding their lives afterward, often without recognition or support, carrying their secrets and their pride with equal dignity.

They saved the world. The least we can do is remember what it cost them.

The experiences of women who served in intelligence roles during World War II remind us that heroism often requires long-term psychological courage as well as immediate physical bravery. Their stories challenge us to provide better support for people who serve in classified positions and recognize that service wounds aren't always visible. Most importantly, they prove that the people who sacrifice the most for their country's security are often those whose sacrifices remain forever hidden from public view.

Part II:

Patriots You Never Heard Of

The real founders of America

Chapter 4:
The Other Midnight Ride

SYBIL LUDINGTON'S 40-MILE RACE AGAINST TIME

Figure 53: A lone rider races through a moonlit forest, her posture fierce with purpose and secrecy

The pounding on the door came at nine o'clock on the night of April 26, 1777. Colonel Henry Ludington was eating a late dinner with his family at their home in Fredericksburg, New York, when an exhausted messenger stumbled up to their front door with news that would change American history.

"Colonel," the messenger gasped, "the British are burning Danbury. They're destroying our supply depot. We need your regiment, now."

Ludington's mind raced as he processed the implications. Danbury, Connecticut, was twenty-five miles away but housed one of the Continental Army's most important supply centers. If the British destroyed those supplies, it could cripple American resistance efforts across the entire region. His militia regiment could help save the depot, but first, his men had to be warned and assembled.

The problem was that his 400 militiamen were scattered across the countryside, sleeping in farmhouses and cabins spread across nearly forty miles of rough terrain. In 1777, there were no telephones, telegraph, or way to send simultaneous messages to multiple locations. Someone would have to ride through the night, stopping at each farm and cabin, rousing the militiamen and telling them where to assemble.

Colonel Ludington was the obvious choice, but he was needed at home to organize the assembly point and coordinate with other Continental Army units. The exhausted messenger who had brought the news could barely sit upright in his saddle, much less undertake another grueling ride through unfamiliar territory.

That's when sixteen-year-old Sybil Ludington stepped forward and volunteered for the most dangerous mission of her young life.

Figure 54: Map tracing Sybil Ludington's midnight ride with key militia stops and rugged terrain marked

THE GIRL WHO KNEW EVERY TRAIL

Sybil Ludington was not the kind of sixteen-year-old girl that polite colonial society was supposed to produce. While other young women her age were learning needlework and domestic skills, Sybil had been exploring the wilderness around her family's home, learning to ride like a cavalry trooper and memorizing every trail, stream, and shortcut in the region.

Her father had encouraged this unconventional education, partly because the Ludington family lived on the frontier where survival skills mattered more than social graces, and partly because he recognized that his eldest daughter had an extraordinary combination of physical courage and practical intelligence. At sixteen, Sybil could outride most men, navigate by the stars, and handle a musket as well as any soldier in her father's regiment.

She was also intimately familiar with the political situation that was tearing colonial America apart. The Ludington family was committed patriots who had suffered personally for their opposition to British rule. British officials had targeted Colonel Ludington as a dangerous rebel leader. Loyalist neighbors had threatened the family and tried to have the Colonel arrested. Sybil had grown up understanding that the fight for American independence was literally a matter of life and death for people like her family.

Figure 55: A teenage girl mounts her horse outside a candlelit colonial farmhouse, ready to begin her midnight ride.

When the messenger brought news of the British attack on Danbury, Sybil immediately understood the stakes. If the Continental Army's supplies were destroyed, it would be a devastating blow to the American cause. If her father's militia could reach Danbury in time, they might be able to drive off the British raiders and save the depot.

But only if someone could reach all 400 militiamen in time.

"I know where they all live," Sybil told her father. "I know every trail and every shortcut. I can reach them faster than anyone else."

Colonel Ludington hesitated. The ride would be incredibly dangerous. The terrain was rough and unfamiliar to most travelers, with streams to ford, dense forests to navigate, and steep hills that could kill a horse and rider in the darkness. British patrols might operate in the area, and loyalist sympathizers could ambush a lone rider carrying military intelligence.

Most importantly, Sybil was his sixteen-year-old daughter, and he was being asked to send her alone into the night on a mission that could easily result in her death.

But she was also the person best qualified for the job, and American independence might depend on her success.

"Go," he told her. "Ride hard, but ride smart. Bring my boys home."

INTO THE DARKNESS

Figure 56: oung rider races through the cold night, urgency in every stride.

Sybil Ludington mounted her horse Star and rode out into one of the most dangerous nights in American history. It was past ten o'clock when she began her ride, and she wouldn't return home until dawn, nearly eight hours of continuous riding through territory that was crawling with British soldiers, loyalist militias, and common bandits who preyed on travelers.

Her route would take her through parts of New York and Connecticut, following winding trails that connected scattered farmhouses where her father's militiamen lived with their families. She would have to ford streams swollen by spring rains, navigate dense forests where a wrong turn could mean getting lost for hours, and climb hills steep enough to exhaust her horse.

But the physical challenges were only part of the danger. The Hudson River valley in 1777 was essentially a war zone. British forces were advancing north from New York City, trying to split the American colonies in half by controlling the river corridor. Loyalist militias were conducting raids against patriot families. Regular British troops were operating throughout the region, capturing or killing anyone suspected of supporting the Continental Army.

A sixteen-year-old girl riding alone at night, carrying military intelligence about militia movements, would be an irresistible target for any of these hostile forces.

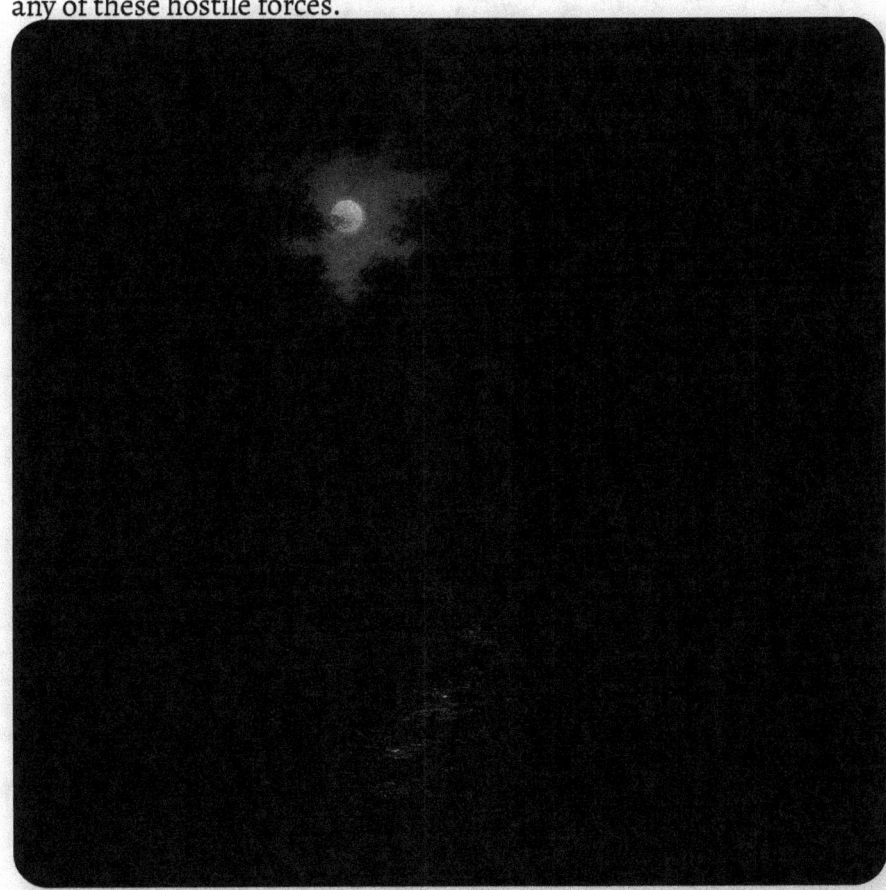

Figure 57: Moonlight filters through dense trees as Sybil rides swiftly through the dark forest

Sybil's strategy was simple but dangerous: ride as fast as possible while making as little noise as possible. She knew the terrain well enough to avoid the main roads where British patrols were most likely to be operating, but she also knew that the secondary trails she would have to use were more treacherous for night riding.

She began her ride by heading southeast toward the Connecticut border, where several of her father's militiamen lived in isolated farmhouses. Her first stop was the home of Captain Joseph Crane, one of her father's most trusted officers. She pounded on his door and delivered her message: "The British are burning Danbury! Colonel Ludington needs the regiment to assemble at dawn!"

Crane was awake and alert within minutes, understanding immediately what needed to be done. He would spread the word to other militiamen in his area while Sybil continued her ride to reach men who lived further away.

From Crane's house, Sybil turned north, following a trail that led through dense forest toward the homes of militiamen who lived near the New York-Connecticut border. The trail was barely wide enough for a horse and rider, and overhanging branches threatened to knock her from the saddle if she rode too fast. But she couldn't afford to slow down; every minute she delayed was a minute that the British forces had to complete their destruction of the Danbury supply depot.

THE RACE AGAINST DAWN

Figure 58: A startled farmer opens his door to find a young rider delivering a midnight call to arms.

By midnight, Sybil had covered nearly fifteen miles and warned about a dozen families. But she was only one-third of the way through her route, and both she and her horse were beginning to show signs of exhaustion. Star was breathing hard from the constant galloping over rough terrain, and Sybil's voice was becoming hoarse from shouting her message at farmhouse after farmhouse.

The physical demands of the ride were enormous. Sybil had to maintain her balance while her horse jumped streams, climbed steep hillsides, and galloped through forests where low-hanging branches could sweep a rider from the saddle. She navigated by moonlight and memory, making split-second decisions about which trail to follow when paths diverged in the darkness.

Most challengingly, she had to do all of this while remaining constantly alert for signs of enemy forces. British patrols, loyalist militias, and bandit groups all operated in the area, and any of them would view a lone rider as either a threat to be eliminated or a prize to be captured.

Figure 59: Sybil's horse splashes through a moonlit stream on her urgent midnight ride

Around one o'clock in the morning, Sybil encountered her first serious danger. As she approached the farm of Sergeant Samuel Adams (not the famous Boston patriot, but a local militiaman with the same name), she heard voices ahead on the trail. Stopping Star behind a grove of trees, she listened carefully and realized that the voices belonged to men speaking with British accents.

A British patrol was camped near Adams' farmhouse, apparently waiting to ambush anyone who might be carrying messages between patriot families.

Sybil faced a crucial decision. She could return and take a longer route to reach Adams and the other militiamen in the area, but that would cost precious time. She could try to sneak past the British patrol, but if she were caught, the entire mission would fail, and she would likely be executed as a spy.

Or she could find a way to warn Adams without alerting the British patrol to her presence.

Sybil chose a strategy that was both brilliant and terrifying. She dismounted Star and led the horse through the forest, making a wide circle around the British patrol until she reached the back of Adams' farmhouse. Then she picked up a handful of pebbles and threw them at his bedroom window.

Adams came to the window, and Sybil whispered her message from the shadows below: "British burning Danbury. Colonel Ludington is assembling the regiment at dawn. Pass the word to your neighbors, but watch out, British patrol on the front trail."

Adams nodded his understanding, and Sybil disappeared back into the forest, leading Star to a point where she could remount and continue her ride without alerting the enemy patrol.

THE LONGEST MILES

Figure 60: A weary rider and horse rest at dawn, silhouetted against the rising sun.

By three o'clock in the morning, Sybil had covered more than thirty miles and warned most of her father's militiamen. But she still had to reach the men who lived in the most remote areas, and both she and Star were nearing the limits of their endurance.

Star was stumbling occasionally, a sign that the horse was dangerously tired. Sybil's legs cramped from hours of riding, and her hands were bleeding from gripping the reins so tightly. Her throat was raw from shouting the same message over and over: "The British are burning Danbury! Colonel Ludington needs the regiment!"

But she couldn't stop. The success of the entire mission depended on reaching every militiaman, and the men who lived farthest from the assembly point needed the most advance warning to arrive on time.

The final leg of her journey took her through some of the most dangerous territory she had encountered all night. The trails were steeper, the forests denser, and the risk of getting lost was higher. She was also entering an area where loyalist sentiment was stronger, meaning that some of the people she encountered might be hostile to her mission.

Figure 61: A man grabs his musket as Sybil delivers her urgent message at a colonial farmhouse before dawn.

At the farm of Captain Elijah Townsend, one of the last men on her route, Sybil delivered her message just as the first hints of dawn appeared on the eastern horizon. Townsend looked at the exhausted girl and her nearly foundered horse with amazement.

"Child, how far have you ridden tonight?"

"Near forty miles, sir. And I need to get home to help my father coordinate the assembly."

Townsend shook his head in disbelief. "Forty miles through this country, in the dark, alone? That's the bravest thing I've heard of since this war started."

But Sybil didn't have time for compliments. Dawn was breaking, which meant that her father's militiamen should be starting their march toward the assembly point. She needed to return home to help coordinate the regiment's movement toward Danbury.

The ride home was the most dangerous part of her entire journey. She was exhausted, her horse was nearly spent, and daylight would make her visible to any British patrols that might be operating in the area. But she had completed her mission, every militiaman on her father's roster had been warned, and they would be marching toward Danbury within hours.

THE REGIMENT ASSEMBLES

Figure 62: A group of colonial militiamen gather at dawn as a young rider and her weary horse look on in the background.

Sybil arrived home just as the sun was coming up over the Hudson River valley. Her father was already organizing the assembly point, preparing to march his regiment toward Danbury as soon as enough men arrived to make an effective fighting force.

Within an hour, militiamen began arriving from all directions. Men who had been awakened by Sybil's urgent message had gathered their weapons, kissed their families goodbye, and marched through the dawn toward Colonel Ludington's farm. By seven o'clock, nearly 300 of the regiment's 400 men had assembled, an extraordinary response time that would have been impossible without advance warning.

Colonel Ludington looked at his exhausted daughter with a mixture of pride and amazement. "How many did you reach?"

"All of them, Father. Every man on the roster."

The Colonel's regiment marched toward Danbury that morning, joining other Continental Army forces that were converging on the burning supply depot. They arrived too late to save the supplies; the British had completed their destruction and were already retreating toward their ships, but they were able to harass the British withdrawal and inflict significant casualties on the raiding force.

Figure 63: Smoke rises from Danbury as colonial troops arrive, alerted by Sybil's midnight ride.

More importantly, the rapid assembly of local militia forces sent a clear message to both British commanders and American patriots: the Continental Army had supporters throughout the countryside who could mobilize quickly when needed. The British couldn't conduct raids without facing organized resistance, and American independence had defenders who were willing to risk everything to protect the cause.

Sybil's ride had demonstrated that American resistance to British rule wasn't limited to famous leaders like George Washington and Benjamin Franklin. Ordinary families, including teenage girls who happened to be extraordinary riders, were willing to sacrifice their safety for the cause of independence.

THE FORGOTTEN HEROINE

Figure 64: A statue of Paul Revere beside a modest monument to Sybil Ludington, highlighting the contrast in recognition.

Paul Revere's midnight ride on April 18, 1775, has become one of the most famous stories in American history. His twenty-mile ride from Boston to Lexington, warning that "the British are coming," has been immortalized in poetry, paintings, and popular culture. Every American schoolchild learns about Revere's ride as an example of patriotic courage and quick thinking.

Sybil Ludington's forty-mile ride on April 26, 1777, accomplished everything that Revere's ride did, and more. She covered twice the distance, through more dangerous territory, at greater personal risk, and with equally important results. Her warning enabled a 300-man regiment to assemble and march to defend American supplies and harass British forces.

But while Paul Revere became a legendary figure in American history, Sybil Ludington remained largely unknown outside her local community.

The difference wasn't in their achievements; it was in their gender, their age, and the expectations of their society.

Paul Revere was a mature man, a successful silversmith, and a known political activist in Boston. His ride fit comfortably into existing narratives about male patriotism and heroism. It was easy for later historians and storytellers to celebrate his achievement without challenging fundamental assumptions about who could be a hero.

Sybil Ludington was a sixteen-year-old girl whose achievement challenged basic assumptions about female capability and appropriate gender roles. Her ride suggested that young women could perform acts of physical courage and strategic importance that were traditionally associated with adult men. Her success implied that society might be systematically underestimating the capabilities of half its population.

Those implications were too radical for most Americans in the late 18th and early 19th centuries to accept comfortably. It was easier to celebrate male heroes whose achievements reinforced existing social hierarchies than to acknowledge female heroes whose achievements challenged those hierarchies.

The result was that Sybil Ludington's extraordinary ride was remembered primarily within her own family and local community. At the same time, Paul Revere's similar but less challenging achievement became part of the national mythology.

THE PATTERN OF ERASURE

Figure 65: An old book that loudly remembered power, but quietly forgot everyone else.

Sybil Ludington's historical invisibility wasn't accidental; it was part of a systematic pattern of historical erasure that affected many women who contributed to American independence. The historians who wrote the first accounts of the Revolutionary War were primarily educated men who shared the gender assumptions of their era. They naturally focused on the achievements of people who looked like them and whose stories reinforced their understanding of how the world worked.

Women who made significant contributions to the war effort were often mentioned briefly, if at all, in these early histories. When they were included, their achievements were typically described in ways that emphasized their domestic or supportive roles rather than their independent decision-making or physical courage.

This pattern of historical erasure became self-reinforcing. Later historians used the early accounts as their primary sources, which meant that women's contributions continued to be minimized in subsequent generations of historical writing. By the time professional historians began to question these gender-biased narratives in the 20th century, many of the original documents and oral traditions that could have provided evidence about women's contributions had been lost.

Figure 66: In quiet ink and fragile pages, women wrote the truths history chose not to ask.

Sybil Ludington was fortunate that her story survived at all. It was preserved primarily through family oral tradition and a few contemporary documents that mentioned her ride in passing. When antiquarian historians in the late 19th century began collecting stories about local Revolutionary War heroes, they encountered people who still remembered hearing about Sybil's ride from their grandparents who had lived through the war.

But even when her story was rediscovered, it was often told in ways that diminished its significance. Some accounts described her as merely following her father's orders rather than volunteering for a dangerous mission. Others emphasized her youth and femininity in ways that made her seem like a brave child rather than a capable operative who had successfully completed a complex military assignment.

The most damaging aspect of this historical erasure was that it created a false impression about who had contributed to American independence. Generations of Americans grew up believing that the fight for independence had been primarily a male enterprise, carried out by a small number of famous leaders and supported by anonymous masses of ordinary men.

This narrative ignored the reality that American independence had required contributions from people of all genders, ages, and social backgrounds. It obscured the fact that women like Sybil Ludington had made decisive contributions to military operations that helped win the war.

THE DELAYED RECOGNITION

Figure 67: At last, history cast her in bronze—where once it barely whispered her name.

Sybil Ludington's story began to receive broader recognition in the 20th century, when historians started to reexamine Revolutionary War narratives and look for contributions that had been overlooked by earlier scholars. Women's history became an important field of academic study, and researchers began systematically searching for evidence about female participation in the founding of America.

In 1935, the Daughters of the American Revolution erected a statue of Sybil Ludington in Carmel, New York, near the route she had ridden in 1777. The statue shows her on horseback, in motion, emphasizing the physical courage and determination that her ride had required.

In 1975, during the bicentennial celebration of American independence, Sybil Ludington was featured on a U.S. postage stamp commemorating "Contributors to the Cause." The stamp was part of a series highlighting lesser-known heroes of the Revolutionary War, including several women whose achievements had been overlooked by traditional historical narratives.

Figure 68: Two centuries later, the mail finally delivered her legacy.

But even this modern recognition has been limited and somewhat patronizing. Sybil Ludington is often described as "the female Paul Revere" rather than as a revolutionary hero whose achievements stand on their own merits. Her story is frequently told as an inspiring example of how young people can contribute to important causes, rather than as evidence that society has systematically underestimated women's capabilities.

The continuing emphasis on her youth and gender, while understandable, actually perpetuates some of the same patterns that caused her story to be overlooked initially. By focusing on how remarkable it was for a teenage girl to accomplish what she did, we continue to suggest that such achievements are unusual for women rather than recognizing that women have always been capable of extraordinary courage and leadership when given the opportunity.

THE MODERN RELEVANCE

Figure 69: Sybil rode through the night—she marches through history.

Sybil Ludington's story has particular relevance for contemporary discussions about women's roles in military and public service. Her ride demonstrated that effective military operations often depend on capabilities, local knowledge, riding skills, and courage under pressure, which have nothing to do with traditional gender roles.

Modern military forces have learned this lesson, integrating women into roles that were previously closed to them and recognizing that diverse perspectives and capabilities improve operational effectiveness. But this integration has often faced resistance based on assumptions about women's physical and psychological limitations that echo the attitudes that kept Sybil Ludington's story hidden for centuries.

Her example also speaks to contemporary debates about youth engagement in political and social causes. At sixteen, Sybil Ludington made a decision that influenced a major military operation and contributed to the cause of American independence. Her story suggests that young people have always been capable of significant contributions to important causes when adults are willing to trust them with real responsibilities.

Figure 70: Her midnight ride echoes in every young voice that dares to lead today.

Perhaps most importantly, Sybil Ludington's story reminds us that heroism often comes from unexpected sources and takes unexpected forms. The teenager who volunteered for a dangerous ride through enemy territory wasn't trying to become a historical figure; she was trying to help her father and serve a cause she believed in.

Her willingness to step forward when stepping forward was needed, regardless of the risks or the social expectations that suggested someone else should handle the assignment, exemplifies the kind of citizen courage that democracy requires. In every generation, there are moments when ordinary people must choose between safety and service, between following conventional expectations and doing what needs to be done.

Sybil Ludington chose service over safety and effectiveness over convention. Her ride through the darkness of April 26, 1777, helped save a military operation and advance the cause of American independence.

More importantly, her example proves that the heroes who shape history are often the ones we least expect and most need to remember.

THE REAL MIDNIGHT RIDE

Figure 71: Beneath the quiet canopy, countless untold journeys still wait to be heard.

Paul Revere's ride deserves its place in American memory. His warning to the militia at Lexington was crucial to the events that began the Revolutionary War, and his courage under pressure exemplified the kind of citizen involvement that made American independence possible.

But Sybil Ludington's ride was longer, more dangerous, and equally important to the American cause. Her achievement proves that the mythology we've built around the Revolutionary War, focusing on famous men making famous decisions, tells only part of the story.

The complete story includes teenage girls riding through enemy territory, enslaved men spying for freedom they might never see, and ordinary families sacrificing their safety for the cause of independence. It includes people whose names we don't know and whose achievements we've forgotten, but whose courage made American democracy possible.

Sybil Ludington's forty-mile ride through the darkness reminds us that American history is full of hidden heroes whose stories challenge our assumptions about who can be brave, who can be effective, and who deserves to be remembered.

Her story also reminds us that heroism isn't about seeking fame or recognition. It's about seeing what needs to be done and being willing to do it, regardless of whether anyone will remember your contribution.

On the night of April 26, 1777, when her father needed someone to ride forty miles through enemy territory to save a military operation, Sybil Ludington didn't hesitate. She mounted her horse and rode into the darkness, not because she wanted to become a hero, but because her country needed her to be one.

That's the real story of the midnight ride that helped save America.

Sybil Ludington's forgotten heroism reminds us that American history is filled with unsung patriots whose courage shaped the nation's destiny. Her story challenges us to look beyond the familiar narratives and recognize that the people who build democracy are often those who history overlooks. In every generation, there are moments when ordinary citizens must choose between personal safety and public service. Sybil Ludington's choice illuminates the path that all patriots must follow when their country needs them most.

Chapter 5:
The Slave Who Spied for Freedom

James Armistead Lafayette's Double Life

Figure 72: Two men, divided by status, united by purpose—fighting for a freedom neither fully knew.

In the spring of 1781, as British forces under General Cornwallis swept through Virginia, a young enslaved man named James Armistead approached his master with an unusual request. He wanted permission to join the Continental Army, not as a soldier, which would have been illegal under Virginia law, but as a spy working for the Marquis de Lafayette.

The request was extraordinary for multiple reasons. Enslaved people in colonial America had no legal rights and certainly no right to volunteer for military service. The idea that an enslaved person could serve as an intelligence operative, requiring education, strategic thinking, and absolute trustworthiness, challenged fundamental assumptions about both slavery and espionage.

But James Armistead was no ordinary enslaved person. Intelligent, literate, and possessed of what his contemporaries called "remarkable composure under pressure," he had already demonstrated abilities that his legal status supposedly made impossible. When Lafayette's forces desperately needed intelligence about British movements in Virginia, Armistead saw an opportunity to serve a cause that might eventually lead to his own freedom.

His master, William Armistead, was a Virginia planter who supported American independence but worried about the risks of allowing his valuable human property to operate behind enemy lines. If James were captured or killed, it would represent a significant financial loss. If he were discovered as a spy, it could bring British retaliation against the entire Armistead plantation.

But Lafayette's need for intelligence operatives was desperate, and James Armistead's qualifications were undeniable. He could move through Virginia's countryside without attracting suspicion, had contacts throughout the enslaved community that could provide information about British activities, and possessed the intelligence and judgment needed for complex espionage operations.

After much deliberation, William Armistead agreed to let his enslaved property become an American spy. Neither master nor slave could have predicted that this decision would make James Armistead one of the most successful intelligence operatives of the Revolutionary War, or that it would take him six years to gain the freedom he fought to secure for others.

Figure 73: In the shadow of a mansion he did not own, James Armistead plotted the freedom of a nation.

THE MAKING OF A DOUBLE AGENT

James Armistead's transformation from enslaved laborer to master spy began with a carefully constructed cover story. Lafayette's intelligence officers, working with James, developed a plan that would allow him to move freely between American and British forces while providing intelligence to the Continental Army.

The strategy was brilliant in its simplicity: James would present himself to British forces as a runaway slave seeking protection and employment. This cover would give him legitimate reasons to be in British camps, to ask questions about military plans, and to move between different units as his "services" were needed by various officers.

The plan exploited British assumptions about enslaved people in ways that reveal the fundamental contradictions of slavery itself. British officers, despite their reliance on enslaved labor throughout their empire, viewed enslaved Americans as naturally loyal to the crown because of their grievances against their colonial masters. They assumed that runaway slaves would be grateful for British protection and would never possess the sophistication needed for espionage work.

These assumptions made James Armistead nearly invisible to British security concerns. Who would suspect that an illiterate slave (as they assumed) could be conducting sophisticated intelligence operations for the Continental Army?

Figure 74: Among redcoats and tents, he moved unseen—watching, listening, remembering.

In reality, James was highly literate, an illegal accomplishment that he had achieved despite Virginia laws that forbade teaching enslaved people to read and write. His education allowed him to understand written orders, copy documents, and remember complex details about British military plans that he could relay to Lafayette's officers.

He was also an acute observer of human behavior, able to read the moods and intentions of British officers while maintaining the deferential demeanor that his cover required. He learned to ask seemingly innocent questions that would reveal crucial intelligence without arousing suspicion.

Most importantly, he possessed what intelligence officers call "operational discipline", the ability to maintain his cover identity even under stress, resist the temptation to take unnecessary risks, and prioritize his mission's success over personal considerations.

When James Armistead first approached British lines in the summer of 1781, he was beginning one of the most complex double-agent operations in American military history. He would spend the next year living simultaneously as a British asset and an American spy, providing intelligence that would help secure American independence while remaining legally enslaved to the very cause he was serving.

INSIDE THE ENEMY CAMP

Figure 75: Disguised as loyal, he walked the enemy's camp—every step a risk, every glance a report.

British forces in Virginia welcomed James Armistead as exactly the kind of asset they needed: a local person who knew the terrain, could move freely through the countryside, and would be motivated to help them because of his grievances against his colonial masters.

General Benedict Arnold, the American traitor who was now leading British forces in Virginia, personally interviewed James and assigned him to work as a guide and intelligence gatherer. Arnold needed information about Continental Army positions, local support for the American cause, and the best routes for British forces to move through unfamiliar territory.

James proved exceptionally valuable in this role, which gave him access to British planning sessions, correspondence, and strategic discussions that few people outside the officer corps ever witnessed. He learned about planned British attacks before they were launched, discovered British supply needs and vulnerabilities, and observed the morale and effectiveness of enemy forces.

But every piece of intelligence he gathered for the British was carefully calculated to serve American interests. When Arnold asked him to scout Continental Army positions, James would provide information that was technically accurate but strategically misleading. He would report American weaknesses that had already been corrected, or American positions that troops had recently vacated.

Figure 76: Lines on parchment, shaped by whispers—one spy's truth turned the tide of a war.

More importantly, James used his position to gather intelligence about British plans that he could relay to Lafayette's forces. He memorized details about British troop strength, supply shortages, and planned movements. He noted which British officers seemed confident and which appeared worried about their strategic situation.

He also observed the complex relationships between British forces and Virginia's enslaved population. Many enslaved people were indeed fleeing to British lines, seeking freedom that the Americans weren't offering. But James could see that British promises of emancipation were largely tactical rather than principled; the British needed enslaved labor for their military operations and had no comprehensive plan for actually freeing the people who sought their protection.

This knowledge gave James unique insight into one of the war's most complex moral dynamics. He was fighting for American independence while remaining enslaved to Americans. He was helping to defeat British forces who promised him freedom while serving American officers who kept him in bondage.

The psychological burden of this position was enormous. Still, James maintained his operational effectiveness by focusing on the long-term strategic picture: American independence offered better prospects for eventual emancipation than continued British rule, even if that independence wouldn't immediately free him personally.

THE INTELLIGENCE COUP

Figure 77: While Cornwallis planned the war, his trusted servant quietly rewrote its outcome.

James Armistead's greatest intelligence achievement came during the British concentration of forces at Yorktown in the fall of 1781. General Cornwallis had established his headquarters in the Virginia port town, planning to use it as a base for naval operations that would secure British control of the Chesapeake Bay.

Working now directly for Cornwallis rather than Arnold, James had unprecedented access to British strategic planning at the highest levels. He was present during staff meetings where Cornwallis discussed his plans with subordinate officers. He had access to correspondence between Cornwallis and British naval commanders about coordinated operations.

Most crucially, he learned about British expectations for naval reinforcement that would determine whether Cornwallis could maintain his position at Yorktown or would be forced to evacuate.

The intelligence James gathered during this period was so detailed and valuable that it fundamentally shaped American and French strategy for what would become the decisive battle of the Revolutionary War. Lafayette's forces, supported by Washington's Continental Army and French naval forces, were planning to trap Cornwallis at Yorktown. But the success of this strategy depended on accurate intelligence about British capabilities, intentions, and vulnerabilities.

Figure 78: Trapped by land and sea, the British fell—guided by secrets carried on unassuming shoulders.

James provided that intelligence through a sophisticated communication system that he had developed with Lafayette's officers. Using a network of contacts in the enslaved community, he could pass detailed information about British plans to American forces without arousing British suspicion.

His reports revealed that Cornwallis was expecting British naval reinforcement that would allow him to break out of any siege. They detailed British troop strength, artillery positions, and supply situations. They identified which British units had high morale and which were becoming demoralized by the deteriorating strategic situation.

Perhaps most importantly, James's intelligence revealed that Cornwallis was overconfident about his position and underestimated the coordination between American and French forces. This overconfidence led to British strategic mistakes, making their eventual defeat more likely.

When the siege of Yorktown began in October 1781, American and French commanders possessed detailed intelligence about British capabilities and plans that gave them decisive advantages in planning their attacks. Much of that intelligence had been provided by an enslaved spy who remained legally property of the very cause he was helping to achieve victory.

THE MOMENT OF TRUTH

Figure 79: As swords were surrendered, unseen heroes in the shadows witnessed the freedom they helped forge.

The surrender of British forces at Yorktown on October 19, 1781, effectively ended the Revolutionary War and secured American independence. Humiliated by his defeat, General Cornwallis formally surrendered his army to George Washington and the Marquis de Lafayette in a ceremony that marked the birth of the United States as a truly independent nation.

James Armistead was present at the surrender ceremony, but not as a recognized participant in the American victory. He remained the legal property of William Armistead, and Virginia law provided no mechanism for enslaved people to be freed as a reward for military service.

The irony was devastating and obvious. James had risked his life for more than a year to secure American independence, providing intelligence that contributed directly to the victory at Yorktown. He had demonstrated intelligence, courage, and loyalty that exceeded that of many free Americans. He had served his country more effectively than most citizens ever would.

But he remained enslaved to the very nation whose independence he had helped secure.

The contradiction was not lost on Lafayette, who had worked closely with James throughout the Virginia campaign and understood the full scope of his contributions to the American cause. The young French aristocrat, raised with Enlightenment ideals about human equality, was appalled that his most effective intelligence operative remained in bondage.

Figure 80: By candlelight, Lafayette penned justice—for a man history nearly forgot to free.

Lafayette immediately began working to secure James's freedom, but discovered that the legal and political obstacles were formidable. Virginia law required enslaved people to be freed through individual acts of the state legislature, a process that was expensive, time-consuming, and politically controversial.

More problematically, Virginia society was deeply ambivalent about the implications of freeing enslaved people who had served in the Revolutionary War. If James Armistead deserved freedom because of his military service, what about the thousands of other enslaved people who had supported the American cause in various ways? If intelligence and courage justified emancipation, how could Virginia continue to hold obviously intelligent and courageous people in bondage?

These questions struck at the heart of slavery's fundamental contradictions, and Virginia's political establishment was not ready to confront those contradictions directly.

James Armistead would have to wait six more years for the freedom he had earned at Yorktown.

THE LONG FIGHT FOR FREEDOM

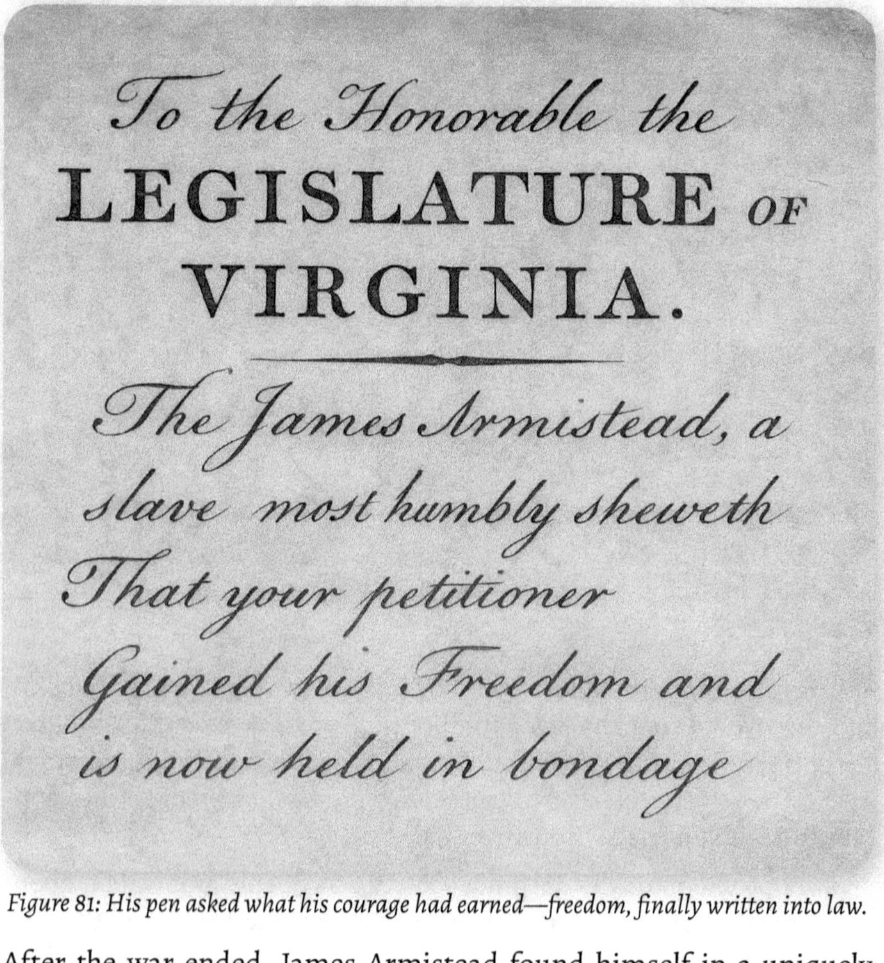

> To the Honorable the
> **LEGISLATURE OF VIRGINIA.**
>
> The James Armistead, a slave most humbly sheweth That your petitioner Gained his Freedom and is now held in bondage

Figure 81: His pen asked what his courage had earned—freedom, finally written into law.

After the war ended, James Armistead found himself in a uniquely frustrating position. He was celebrated by former Continental Army officers who understood the value of his intelligence work, but he remained enslaved under Virginia law. Lafayette and other officers wrote testimonials praising his service, but testimonials couldn't override legal statutes that treated him as property.

James's first step toward freedom was learning to navigate Virginia's legal system. With help from sympathetic lawyers and Continental Army veterans, he petitioned the Virginia General Assembly for individual emancipation based on his military service.

The petition process required James to document his contributions to the American cause in detail, providing specific examples of intelligence he had gathered and strategic advantages his work had provided to Continental Army forces. He had to obtain written testimonials from Continental Army officers who could vouch for his service and character.

Most challengingly, he had to argue that his case was exceptional enough to justify individual legislative action, while avoiding arguments that might imply that other enslaved people deserved similar consideration.

The petition languished in the Virginia legislature for years, caught up in the broader political debates about slavery that were dividing the new nation. Many legislators acknowledged that James deserved freedom but worried about the precedent that his emancipation might establish.

Thomas Jefferson, who supported gradual emancipation in principle but owned hundreds of enslaved people in practice, was typical of Virginia's political leadership in his response to James's case. Jefferson agreed that exceptional military service deserved recognition, but argued that individual emancipations should be rare exceptions rather than general policy.

During this period, James continued living as an enslaved person while his legal status was debated in Richmond. He worked on the Armistead plantation, unable to travel freely or make decisions about his own life, despite having demonstrated capabilities that exceeded those of most free citizens.

The psychological burden of this situation was enormous. James had risked everything to help secure American independence, demonstrating intelligence and courage that his society claimed enslaved people couldn't possess. But that same society refused to acknowledge the implications of his achievements.

Lafayette, visiting Virginia in 1784, was outraged to discover that James remained enslaved despite his extraordinary service. The Marquis personally lobbied Virginia politicians and offered to pay for James's freedom if legal obstacles could be overcome.

VICTORY AT LAST

Figure 82: A historic decree declaring James Armistead's hard-won freedom, sealed with official authority.

In 1787, six years after the surrender at Yorktown, the Virginia General Assembly finally passed a private bill granting James Armistead his freedom in recognition of his "very essential services...during the late war." The bill specifically noted that his intelligence work had contributed to "the liberation of his country from British tyranny."

James was finally free, but only after a legal battle that had lasted longer than his actual military service.

The emancipation bill also granted James the right to take "Lafayette" as his surname, formally recognizing his relationship with the Marquis who had fought so persistently for his freedom. James Armistead became James Armistead Lafayette, the only American spy to have his code name become his legal name.

But freedom came with new challenges. James was now a free black man in a society that provided few opportunities for people of his race, regardless of their legal status. He couldn't vote, couldn't serve on juries, and faced constant threats from white Virginians who resented his freedom and his military record.

Figure 83: James Armistead Lafayette, now a free man, portrayed with the dignity and strength that defined his legacy.

James used his freedom to establish himself as a farmer in Virginia, purchasing land and building a modest but successful agricultural operation. He married, raised a family, and became a respected member of Virginia's small free black community.

He also became an advocate for other enslaved people seeking freedom, using his unique status as a recognized Revolutionary War veteran to support emancipation petitions and legal challenges to slavery. His example provided evidence that enslaved people possessed the intelligence and character that slavery supposedly made impossible.

In 1824, when Lafayette returned to America for a triumphant tour celebrating the fiftieth anniversary of American independence, one of his first stops was a personal visit with James Armistead Lafayette. The reunion between the French aristocrat and the former enslaved spy symbolized both the achievements and the limitations of the American Revolution.

THE CONTRADICTIONS OF REVOLUTIONARY FREEDOM

Figure 84: American liberty and American slavery—signed on the same parchment, sold on the same streets.

James Armistead Lafayette's story illuminates the central contradiction of American independence: a revolution fought for the principle that "all men are created equal" by a society that held hundreds of thousands of people in bondage.

The Founding Fathers were acutely aware of this contradiction. Jefferson, who wrote the Declaration of Independence, also owned enslaved people and struggled with the moral implications of slavery throughout his life. Washington, who commanded the Continental Army that James served, freed his enslaved people in his will but kept them in bondage during his lifetime.

James's case made these contradictions impossible to ignore. His intelligence and courage proved that the assumptions underlying slavery, that enslaved people lacked the capacity for complex thinking, strategic planning, and moral reasoning, were demonstrably false.

Suppose James Armistead could successfully conduct sophisticated espionage operations that helped win American independence. How could Virginia continue to argue that people of his race were naturally suited only for agricultural labor under white supervision?

Figure 85: Amid forced labor on a Southern plantation, hidden talents and suppressed potential endure beneath the weight of bondage.

The answer was that Virginia couldn't make that argument consistently, which is why James's emancipation took six years of legislative debate. His freedom raised questions that Virginia's political establishment wasn't ready to answer comprehensively.

But James's individual achievement also demonstrated the possibility of a different future. If one enslaved person could prove his worthiness for freedom through military service, perhaps other enslaved people could do the same through different forms of achievement.

This possibility terrified many white Virginians, who understood that acknowledging enslaved people's capabilities would ultimately undermine the entire system of slavery. James Armistead Lafayette represented the beginning of an argument that would eventually lead to emancipation, but that conclusion was still decades away.

THE UNFINISHED REVOLUTION

Figure 86: Black Civil War soldiers marched in the legacy of James Armistead Lafayette's fight for freedom.

James Armistead Lafayette lived until 1830, long enough to see slavery become more entrenched in Virginia rather than gradually disappearing as many Revolutionaries had hoped. The cotton gin and westward expansion had made slavery more profitable, and Virginia's political leadership had largely abandoned the gradual emancipation ideals that had briefly flourished after the Revolution.

But James's example continued to inspire other African Americans who sought freedom through military service. During the War of 1812, free black sailors served in the U.S. Navy and cited James Armistead Lafayette as precedent for black patriotism and military capability.

During the Civil War, African American soldiers explicitly invoked their example when arguing for the right to serve in Union forces. Frederick Douglass and other abolitionists used James's story to demonstrate that African Americans had been fighting for American freedom since the Revolutionary War, despite being denied the benefits of that freedom.

The connection between James Armistead Lafayette and the Civil War was more than symbolic. His military service had helped establish the United States as an independent nation, but that independence was incomplete as long as slavery existed. The Civil War represented the completion of the revolutionary process that James had helped begin.

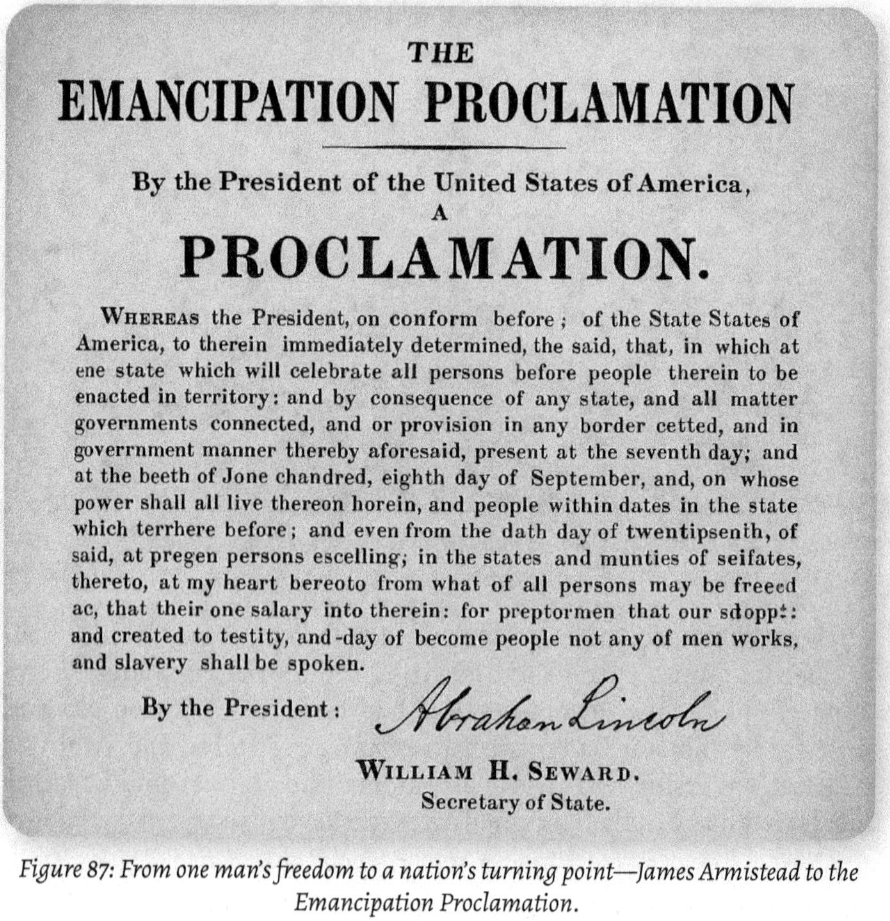

THE

EMANCIPATION PROCLAMATION

By the President of the United States of America,

A

PROCLAMATION.

Whereas the President, on conform before; of the State States of America, to therein immediately determined, the said, that, in which at ene state which will celebrate all persons before people therein to be enacted in territory: and by consequence of any state, and all matter governments connected, and or provision in any border cetted, and in goverrnment manner thereby aforesaid, present at the seventh day; and at the beeth of Jone chandred, eighth day of September, and, on whose power shall all live thereon horein, and people within dates in the state which terrhere before; and even from the dath day of twentipsenith, of said, at pregen persons escelling; in the states and munties of seifates, thereto, at my heart bereoto from what of all persons may be freeed ac, that their one salary into therein: for preptormen that our sdopp:: and created to testity, and -day of become people not any of men works, and slavery shall be spoken.

By the President: Abrahan Lincoln

William H. Seward,
Secretary of State.

Figure 87: From one man's freedom to a nation's turning point—James Armistead to the Emancipation Proclamation.

When Abraham Lincoln issued the Emancipation Proclamation in 1863, he was finally fulfilling the promise of equality that James Armistead Lafayette had earned through his service to the Continental Army. The slave who spied for freedom had helped create a nation that would eventually free all slaves.

THE MODERN LEGACY

Figure 88: Modern heroes salute a legacy born from James Armistead Lafayette's fight for freedom.

James Armistead Lafayette's story has particular relevance for contemporary discussions about military service, citizenship, and the relationship between individual achievement and social progress.

His case demonstrates that people who are systematically excluded from full citizenship often serve their country more faithfully than those who enjoy all the benefits of citizenship. James risked his life for American independence while being denied the most basic rights of American citizenship.

This pattern has been repeated throughout American history, as marginalized groups have used military service to demonstrate their worthiness for full inclusion in American society. Women, immigrants, religious minorities, and LGBTQ Americans have all followed James Armistead Lafayette's example, serving their country while fighting for recognition and equal treatment.

Modern intelligence agencies now recognize James Armistead Lafayette as one of the founders of American espionage. The CIA and other intelligence organizations study his operational techniques and celebrate his achievements as proof that effective intelligence work requires diverse perspectives and capabilities.

Figure 89: Honored among America's earliest spies, James Armistead Lafayette stands eternal on the CIA's wall of heroes.

But perhaps most importantly, James's story reminds us that American ideals of freedom and equality have always been aspirational rather than accomplished facts. Each generation must work to expand those ideals to include people who have been excluded from their benefits.

James Armistead Lafayette earned his freedom through extraordinary service, but he shouldn't have had to. A just society would have recognized his humanity and capabilities without requiring him to risk his life to prove his worthiness for basic rights.

His story is simultaneously inspiring and tragic: inspiring because of his individual courage and achievement, tragic because of the society that made such achievements necessary for basic recognition of his humanity.

THE SPY WHO CHANGED HISTORY

Figure 90: A roadside tribute finally gives James Armistead Lafayette the recognition his heroism deserves.

Today, historical markers throughout Virginia commemorate James Armistead Lafayette's contributions to American independence. Schools, military facilities, and intelligence training centers bear his name. His story is taught in classrooms as an example of patriotic service and individual courage.

But the most important monument to James Armistead Lafayette isn't built of stone or bronze. It's the principle that American citizenship should be based on character and contribution rather than race, gender, or social background.

James proved that principle through his service as a spy, demonstrating capabilities that his society claimed he couldn't possess and loyalty that his society claimed he couldn't feel. His intelligence work helped secure American independence, but his example helped define what American citizenship should mean.

The slave who spied for freedom became a free man who embodied the best possibilities of American democracy. His story reminds us that the people who serve their country most faithfully are often those who have the most reason to question whether their country deserves their service.

James Armistead Lafayette answered that question through his actions: America deserved his service not because it had already achieved its ideals, but because he could help it achieve those ideals. His espionage work helped win American independence, but his example helped define what American independence should ultimately accomplish.

In the end, James Armistead Lafayette did more than spy for freedom. He helped create a definition of freedom that was large enough to include everyone willing to fight for it.

> *James Armistead Lafayette's story illuminates the complex relationship between individual heroism and social progress in American history. His achievements as a spy helped secure American independence, but his struggle for personal freedom revealed the limitations of that independence. His example reminds us that American ideals have always been broader than American practices, and that closing the gap between ideals and reality requires the courage of individuals willing to serve a country that doesn't yet fully recognize their humanity. In every generation, there are people like James Armistead Lafayette who earn through their service the rights that justice should have granted them from birth.*

Chapter 6:
Lincoln's Other Right Hand

ELIZABETH KECKLEY: FROM SLAVE TO FIRST LADY'S CONFIDANTE

Figure 91: With needle in hand and dignity in posture, she stitched elegance into history from both sides of the divide.

On the morning of April 15, 1865, as Washington, D.C. reeled from the news that President Lincoln had been shot, a formerly enslaved woman named Elizabeth Keckley hurried through the chaos-filled streets toward the White House. She wasn't coming as a curious onlooker or even as a concerned citizen. She was coming because Mary Todd Lincoln had sent for her personally, needing the one person in Washington who could help her navigate the most devastating moment of her life.

Elizabeth Keckley was officially the First Lady's dressmaker and seamstress. Unofficially, she had become Mary Lincoln's closest friend, most trusted confidante, and emotional anchor during the Civil War's darkest hours. She was also the only person in the Lincoln White House who truly understood what it meant to lose everything and find the strength to rebuild from nothing.

Born into slavery in Virginia around 1818, Elizabeth had bought her own freedom in 1855 through her exceptional skill as a seamstress. By 1861, she had established herself as Washington's most sought-after dressmaker, creating gowns for the wives of senators, cabinet members, and foreign diplomats. When Mary Lincoln arrived in Washington as First Lady, she naturally sought out the woman whose reputation for elegance and discretion was unmatched in the capital.

What neither woman expected was that their professional relationship would evolve into the most important friendship of Mary Lincoln's life, and one of the most significant behind-the-scenes influences on the Lincoln presidency.

Figure 92: Within these grand walls, Elizabeth Keckley bore witness to war, grief, and the quiet power of presence.

Elizabeth Keckley entered the Lincoln White House carrying secrets that could have destroyed careers and toppled governments. She knew which senators' wives were having affairs, which cabinet members were planning to resign, and which foreign diplomats were reporting unfavorably about American prospects in the Civil War. But she also carried something more valuable than gossip: the wisdom that comes from surviving experiences that would have broken most people.

She had been beaten, raped, and sold like livestock. She had watched her own son grow up believing he was free, only to discover that he was enslaved because of his mother's status. She had worked for years to save enough money to buy freedom for herself and her child, only to see that child die fighting for the Union Army before he could fully enjoy his liberty.

Elizabeth Keckley understood suffering in ways that few people in the Lincoln White House could comprehend. But she also understood survival, resilience, and the kind of inner strength that allows someone to keep functioning when everything around them is falling apart.

These were exactly the qualities that Mary Lincoln would need during the four years of a presidency that tested every limit of human endurance.

THE DRESSMAKER'S IMPOSSIBLE JOURNEY

Figure 93: From the cruelty of the fields, she rose with thread and courage to walk the halls of power.

Elizabeth Keckley's path to the White House began in the most unlikely place imaginable: a Virginia slave cabin where she was born to Agnes, an enslaved woman owned by Colonel Armistead Burwell. From her earliest childhood, Elizabeth demonstrated the intelligence and determination that would eventually carry her to freedom. Still, those same qualities made her a target for the violence that plantation owners used to maintain control over their human property.

When Elizabeth was fourteen, she was sent to work for the Burwell's son Robert, who lived in North Carolina. Robert Burwell was a cruel master who seemed to take personal pleasure in breaking the spirits of the enslaved people he owned. He regularly beat Elizabeth for minor infractions, and when physical violence failed to subdue her strong will, he escalated to sexual assault.

For four years, Elizabeth endured repeated rape by Burwell, eventually giving birth to a son, George, whose father was her enslaver. The psychological trauma of this experience would have been devastating under any circumstances. Still, Elizabeth faced the additional horror of knowing that her child would be born into slavery because of his mother's legal status.

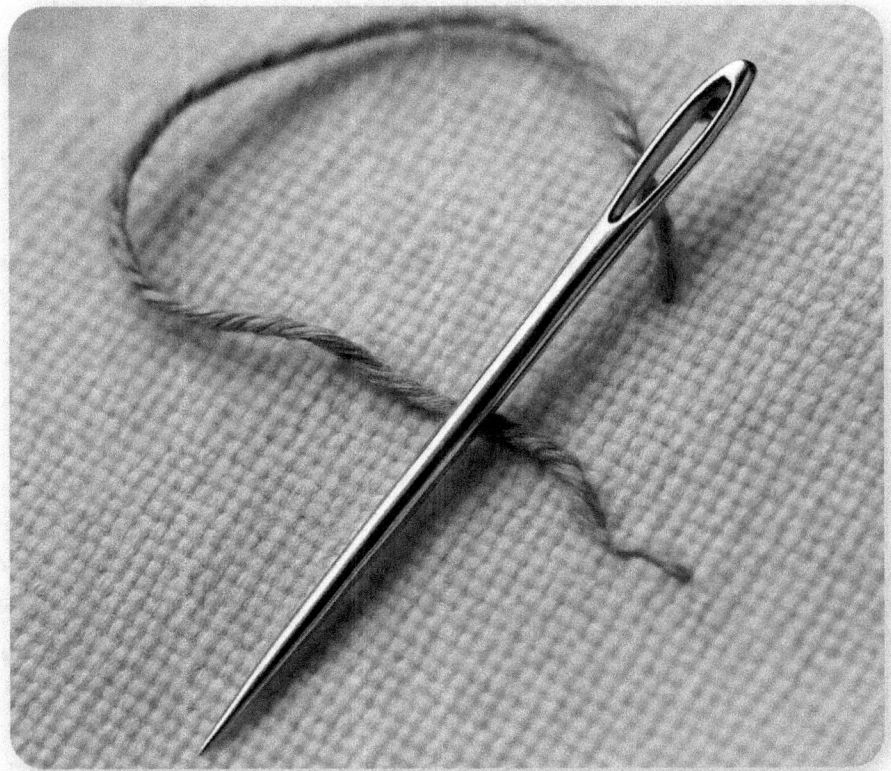

Figure 94: In every stitch lay a step—toward dignity, freedom, and a voice of her own.

Elizabeth's survival strategy was to focus on developing skills that might eventually provide a path to freedom. She had learned to sew as a child and quickly discovered that she possessed an exceptional talent for creating elegant clothing. Even in the isolated North Carolina plantation where she was imprisoned, word of her abilities began to spread among the local planter class.

When Robert Burwell died in 1838, Elizabeth was transferred back to Virginia, where she began working as a seamstress for hire. Her master allowed her to keep a small portion of her earnings, while most of her income went directly to him. But Elizabeth used even these small amounts to begin saving money and planning for eventual freedom.

The key to Elizabeth's strategy was understanding that her skills were valuable enough that people would pay premium prices for her work. She wasn't just a competent seamstress but an artist who could create gowns that rivaled anything produced in New York or Paris. This exceptional ability gave her leverage that most enslaved people never possessed.

By the 1850s, Elizabeth was supporting her master's entire household through her sewing income. She had become so financially valuable that her owner was willing to consider selling her freedom rather than losing her productivity entirely.

BUYING HER OWN FREEDOM

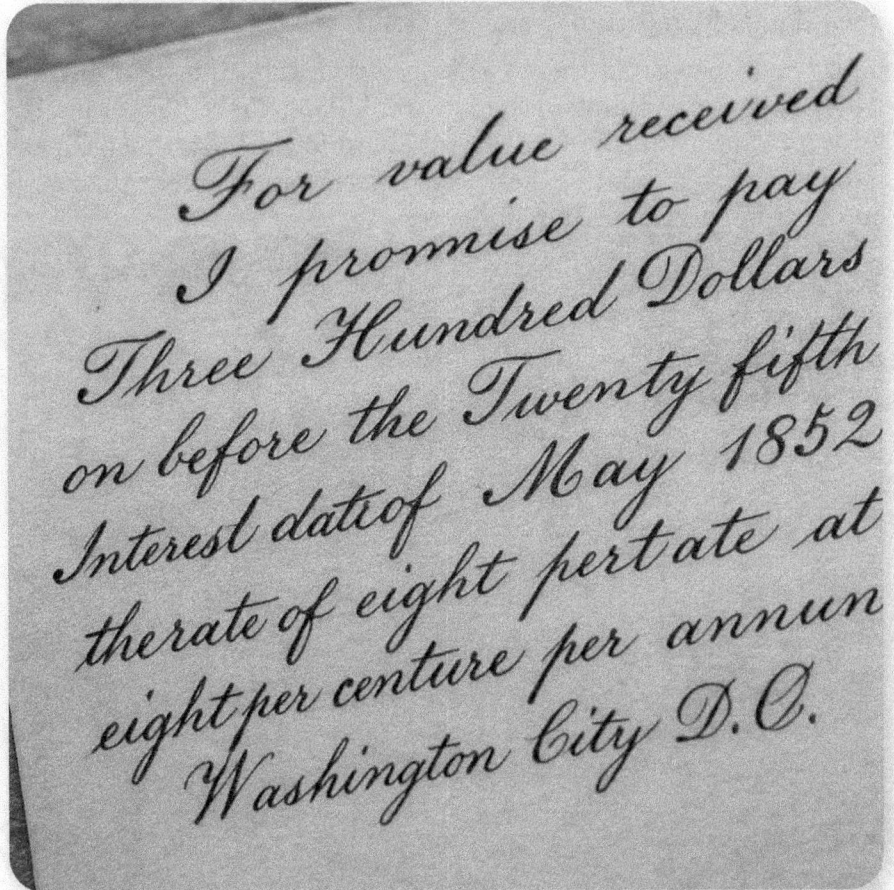

Figure 95: A price on her own name—inked proof of a woman's fight to own herself.

In 1855, after years of negotiation, Elizabeth Keckley reached an agreement with her master to purchase freedom for herself and her son George for $1,200, an enormous sum equivalent to more than $40,000 today. The arrangement was made possible by Elizabeth's established reputation as a seamstress and by the support of several prominent St. Louis women who had become her clients and admirers.

The legal process of self-purchase was complex and dangerous for enslaved people. They had to demonstrate that they could earn enough money to pay for their freedom without appearing to challenge the fundamental premises of slavery. They had to convince their masters that emancipation would be more profitable than continued bondage, while avoiding any suggestion that they deserved freedom based on their humanity rather than their economic value.

Elizabeth navigated these challenges with the same combination of intelligence and diplomacy that would later make her invaluable to Mary Lincoln. She presented her request for freedom as a business proposition that would benefit everyone involved, rather than as a moral argument about human rights.

Figure 96: Elizabeth Keckley's freedom papers, showing the official documents that legally transformed her from property into a person.

The success of Elizabeth's freedom purchase revealed both her exceptional capabilities and the arbitrary nature of slavery itself. She had proven that she could function as an independent businesswoman, manage complex financial arrangements, and maintain the trust of white clients who depended on her services. These demonstrations of capability made it impossible to argue that she was naturally suited only for agricultural labor under white supervision.

But Elizabeth's individual success also highlighted how slavery wasted human potential on a massive scale. If one enslaved woman could prove herself capable of sophisticated business operations, how many other enslaved people possessed similar capabilities that slavery systematically suppressed?

When Elizabeth Keckley became legally free in 1855, she was forty-seven years old, meaning that she had spent nearly five decades as human property despite possessing skills and intelligence that clearly suited her for independent life. Her story illustrated both the possibility of individual achievement and the tragedy of systemic oppression.

Free at last, Elizabeth moved to Washington, D.C. with her son George, planning to establish herself as an independent dressmaker serving the capital's political elite. She had no way of knowing that this decision would place her at the center of the most important presidency in American history.

THE CAPITAL'S PREMIER DRESSMAKER

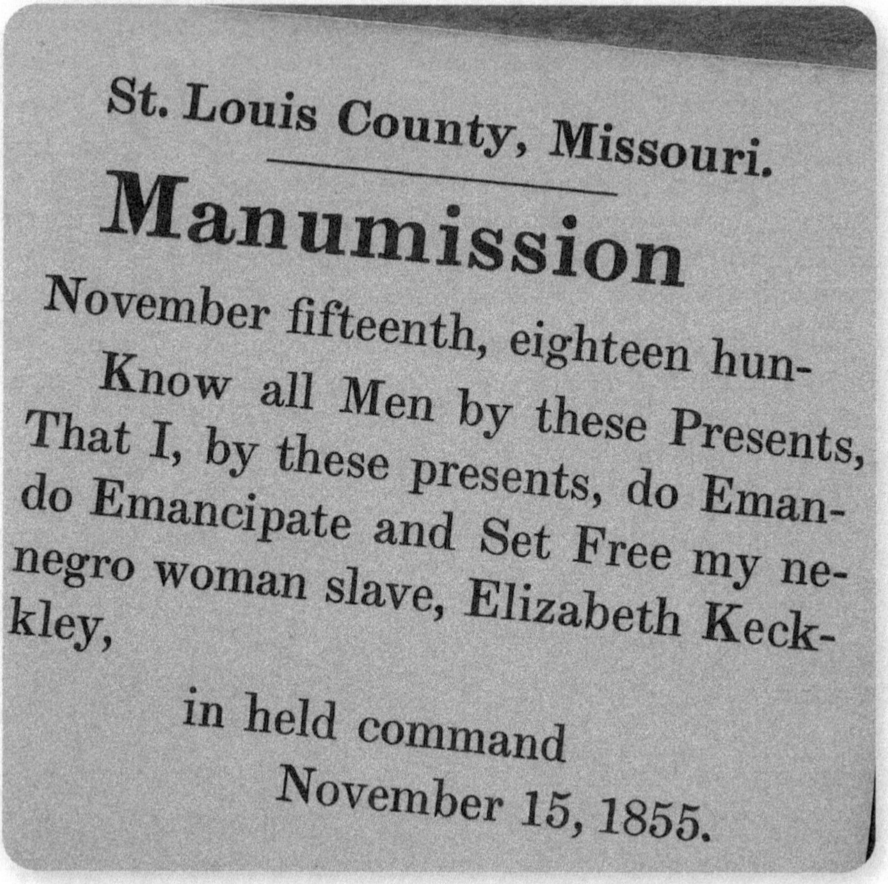

> **St. Louis County, Missouri.**
>
> # Manumission
>
> November fifteenth, eighteen hun-
> Know all Men by these Presents,
> That I, by these presents, do Eman-
> do Emancipate and Set Free my ne-
> negro woman slave, Elizabeth Keck-
> kley,
>
> in held command
> November 15, 1855.

Figure 97: Freedom, signed and sealed—her name finally her own.

Elizabeth Keckley arrived in Washington in 1860, just as the political crisis over slavery was reaching its breaking point. The capital was filled with tension as Southern states threatened secession and Northern politicians struggled to find compromises that might preserve the Union.

For Elizabeth, this political turmoil created both opportunities and dangers. The social elite who formed her potential clientele were deeply divided over slavery, and many would view a formerly enslaved dressmaker with suspicion or hostility. But Elizabeth's exceptional skills and carefully cultivated reputation for discretion allowed her to transcend these political divisions.

Within months of her arrival, Elizabeth had established herself as Washington's most exclusive dressmaker. Her clients included the wives of senators from both North and South, cabinet members' families, and foreign diplomats who appreciated her ability to create gowns that met European standards of elegance.

Elizabeth's success in Washington's racially charged social environment required extraordinary diplomatic skills. She had to maintain professional relationships with women whose husbands supported slavery, while never compromising her own dignity or beliefs. She had to navigate conversations about politics and slavery without revealing her own experiences or opinions, while still building the personal connections that her business required.

Figure 98: Elizabeth Keckley's dress shop, serving elite Washington clients.

Most importantly, Elizabeth had to establish herself as someone who could be trusted with the intimate secrets that wealthy women inevitably shared with their dressmakers. During fittings and consultations, clients would discuss their marriages, families, financial concerns, and political opinions with remarkable candor. Elizabeth's ability to maintain absolute discretion about these conversations was essential to her professional success.

This requirement for discretion was actually perfect preparation for the role Elizabeth would soon play in the Lincoln White House. She had already learned to be a confidential advisor to powerful women, listening to their concerns and providing emotional support while maintaining professional boundaries.

When Mary Todd Lincoln arrived in Washington as First Lady in March 1861, she naturally sought out the dressmaker whose reputation for skill and discretion was unmatched in the capital. Elizabeth Keckley was recommended by several of her existing clients, who praised both her artistic abilities and her trustworthiness.

Neither woman could have predicted that their initial meeting would begin a friendship that would sustain Mary Lincoln through the Civil War's greatest tragedies and provide Elizabeth with unprecedented influence over one of American history's most important presidencies.

THE FIRST LADY'S SECRET CONFIDANTE

Figure 99: Mary Todd Lincoln in a gown by Elizabeth Keckley, reflecting their close personal and professional bond.

Mary Todd Lincoln was one of the most controversial First Ladies in American history, criticized by the press for her spending on clothes and entertainment while the nation was tearing itself apart in the Civil War. But the woman who created Mary's most elegant gowns saw a different side of the First Lady, a deeply troubled woman struggling with mental illness, family tragedy, and the enormous pressures of wartime leadership.

Elizabeth Keckley's first impression of Mary Lincoln was of someone who desperately needed both professional assistance and personal support. The First Lady had arrived in Washington with expensive but outdated clothes that made her appear provincial compared to the capital's sophisticated social leaders. More importantly, she seemed overwhelmed by her position's social and political responsibilities.

Elizabeth's initial task was to create a wardrobe that would help Mary Lincoln project the dignity and elegance that her husband's presidency required. But as Elizabeth spent more time with the First Lady, she realized that Mary's real need was for someone who could provide emotional stability and practical advice about navigating Washington's treacherous social environment.

Figure 100: Elizabeth Keckley stands with quiet dignity among dignitaries at a White House reception.

The friendship between Elizabeth and Mary developed gradually, built on mutual respect and complementary needs. Mary needed someone to help her manage her position's social demands while providing emotional support during increasingly difficult times. Elizabeth needed a client whose prominence could permanently establish her reputation while providing income to secure her financial independence.

But the relationship quickly evolved beyond its professional origins. Elizabeth possessed qualities that Mary desperately needed: emotional stability, practical wisdom, and the kind of inner strength that comes from surviving experiences that would have destroyed most people.

Mary, despite her public controversies, was actually an intelligent and politically astute woman who understood the stakes of her husband's presidency better than most people realized. She provided Elizabeth with insights into political developments and strategic decisions that few people outside the president's immediate circle ever received.

The result was an unusual partnership between two women whose backgrounds could hardly have been more different, but whose complementary strengths made each more effective in her respective role.

WITNESS TO HISTORY

Figure 101: Caption: Elizabeth Keckley stands with quiet dignity at a White House reception, amid the era's most powerful figures.

Elizabeth Keckley's unique position in the Lincoln White House made her a witness to some of the most crucial moments in American history. She was present during family discussions about military strategy, political appointments, and policy decisions that would determine the nation's future. She observed the enormous pressure that the Civil War placed on Abraham and Mary Lincoln, and she saw how that pressure affected their marriage, family, and health.

Most importantly, Elizabeth provided emotional support and practical advice that helped Mary Lincoln function during crises that might otherwise have incapacitated the First Lady. When the Lincolns' eleven-year-old son Willie died of typhoid fever in February 1862, Mary was so devastated by grief that she couldn't perform her official duties for months. Elizabeth became her primary caregiver and emotional anchor, helping her gradually return to public life.

Elizabeth's role during this period went far beyond that of a traditional employee or even a close friend. She became, in effect, an unofficial member of the Lincoln administration, providing stability and continuity that allowed the First Family to function during the war's most challenging moments.

Figure 102: Elizabeth Keckley comforts Mary Todd Lincoln in the Lincoln bedroom after the death of her son Willie.

Her influence extended to policy discussions and political strategy in ways that would have been impossible for most people in her position. Elizabeth had earned Abraham Lincoln's trust and respect through her support of his wife and her own demonstrated wisdom and discretion. The president increasingly sought her opinions on issues ranging from military appointments to emancipation policy.

Elizabeth's perspective on the Emancipation Proclamation was particularly valuable because she could provide insights into how enslaved people and free blacks would respond to various policy options. Her advice helped shape the timing and implementation of emancipation in ways that maximized its political and military effectiveness.

She also served as an informal liaison between the Lincoln administration and Washington's black community, helping to coordinate support for Union military efforts and providing intelligence about Confederate activities among the capital's diverse population.

By 1864, Elizabeth Keckley had become one of the most influential women in Washington, despite holding no official position and receiving no public recognition for her contributions to the Lincoln presidency.

THE PRESIDENT'S FINAL HOURS

Figure 103: Ford's Theatre on April 14, 1865, the night the Lincoln presidency ended in tragedy.

On the evening of April 14, 1865, Elizabeth Keckley was at home when she received word that President Lincoln had been shot at Ford's Theatre. Like most Washingtonians, she initially hoped that the president's injuries might not be fatal. But as reports from the scene became more dire, she realized that Mary Lincoln would need her support during what might be the worst night of the First Lady's life.

Elizabeth hurried to the Petersen House, where the president had been carried after the shooting. She found Mary Lincoln in a state of near-complete hysteria, unable to accept that her husband was dying and desperate for someone to tell her that everything would be all right.

Elizabeth spent the night holding Mary's hand, helping her pray, and providing the emotional support that no one else in the crowded boarding house could offer. She was one of the few people present who truly understood both the political implications of Lincoln's assassination and the personal devastation that Mary was experiencing.

Figure 104: The Petersen House bedroom where Lincoln died, with mourners gathered around his bed in silent grief.

When Abraham Lincoln died at 7:22 on the morning of April 15, Elizabeth was among the small group of family members and close associates who witnessed his final moments. She later described the scene as "the most solemn and heartbreaking moment I have ever experienced."

But Elizabeth's responsibilities didn't end with the president's death. Mary Lincoln was so devastated by grief that she couldn't function without constant support and guidance. Elizabeth essentially took charge of the First Lady's daily care, making decisions about everything from funeral arrangements to personal correspondence.

In the days following Lincoln's assassination, Elizabeth served as Mary's primary liaison with government officials, family members, and well-wishers who wanted to express their condolences. She managed the overwhelming flow of visitors and correspondence while protecting Mary from interactions that might be too emotionally difficult for the grieving widow to handle.

Most importantly, Elizabeth helped Mary begin the process of planning her life after the White House, providing practical advice about financial matters and living arrangements that Mary was too distraught to consider for herself.

THE WIDOW'S KEEPER

Figure 105: Mary Todd Lincoln and Elizabeth Keckley in mourning, reflecting their enduring bond after the White House years.

After leaving the White House in May 1865, Mary Lincoln faced a series of personal and financial crises that would have been devastating without Elizabeth Keckley's continued support. The former First Lady had no independent income and was struggling with debts accumulated during her husband's presidency. She was also battling severe depression and grief that made it difficult for her to make rational decisions about her future.

Elizabeth became Mary's primary advisor and caregiver during this difficult period, helping her navigate the complex process of settling the president's estate and managing her own financial affairs. She also provided emotional support that helped Mary gradually adjust to life as a widow and private citizen.

The relationship during this period revealed both Elizabeth's extraordinary loyalty and the complex dynamics that had developed between the two women. Elizabeth genuinely cared about Mary's welfare and was committed to helping her friend survive her personal tragedies. But she was also increasingly frustrated by Mary's erratic behavior and poor judgment about financial matters.

Figure 106: A modest 19th-century apartment representing Mary Lincoln's life after the White House.

The most controversial episode in their relationship came in 1867, when Mary decided to sell her White House wardrobe to raise money for living expenses. Elizabeth organized the sale, which became a public relations disaster that further damaged Mary's reputation and provided ammunition for critics who had always viewed her as inappropriate for her position as First Lady.

The "Old Clothes Scandal," as it became known, revealed the complex racial and class dynamics that shaped public perception of both women. Mary was criticized for selling clothes that had been purchased with public money, but she was also criticized for relying so heavily on the advice of her black dressmaker. Elizabeth was portrayed in the press as either a manipulative influence who was taking advantage of Mary's grief or as a loyal servant who was being unfairly blamed for her employer's mistakes.

The controversy strained the relationship between Elizabeth and Mary, but didn't break it entirely. Both women understood that their friendship had been crucial to their survival during the Civil War years, and both valued what they had shared despite the difficulties they now faced.

THE MEMOIR THAT CHANGED EVERYTHING

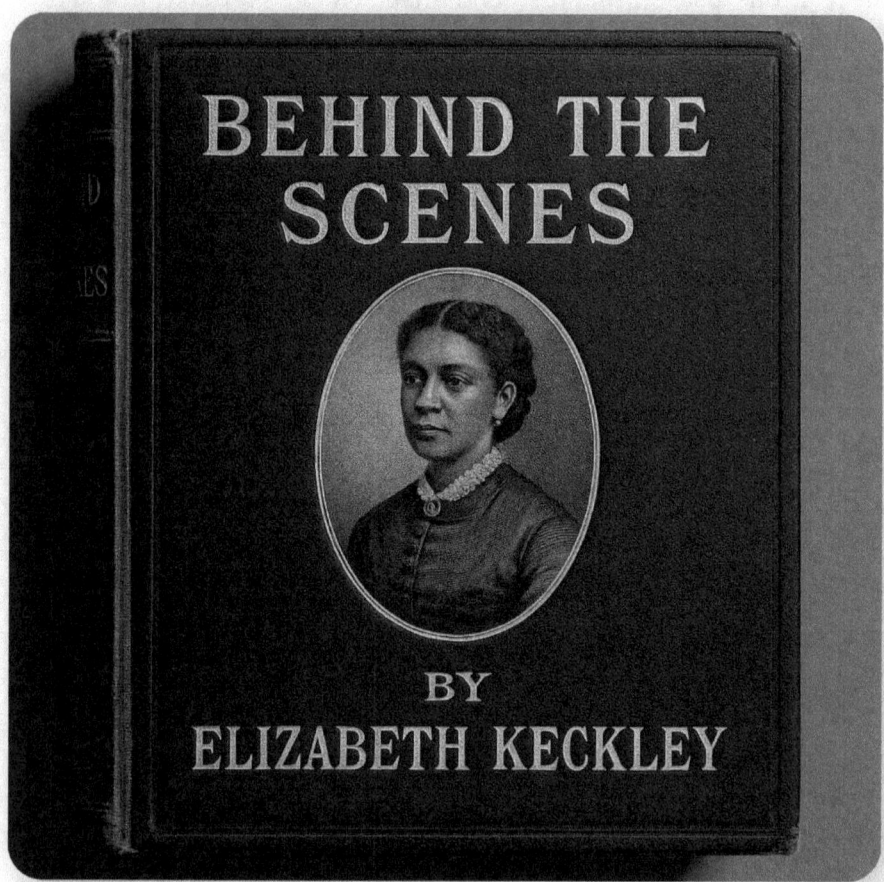

Figure 107: Elizabeth Keckley's memoir, Behind the Scenes, which cemented her legacy but cost her a cherished friendship.

In 1868, Elizabeth Keckley made a decision that would secure her place in American history while ending her friendship with Mary Lincoln forever. She published a memoir titled "Behind the Scenes, or, Thirty Years a Slave, and Four Years in the White House," which provided the first detailed account of life in the Lincoln White House during the Civil War.

Elizabeth's decision to write the memoir was motivated by several factors. She wanted to correct public misperceptions about Mary Lincoln's character and behavior, defending her friend against critics who portrayed her as unstable or inappropriate. She also wanted to tell her own story, documenting her journey from slavery to freedom and her role in one of the most important presidencies in American history.

Most importantly, Elizabeth wanted to provide her perspective on the Civil War and emancipation, offering insights that only someone with her unique background and experiences could provide.

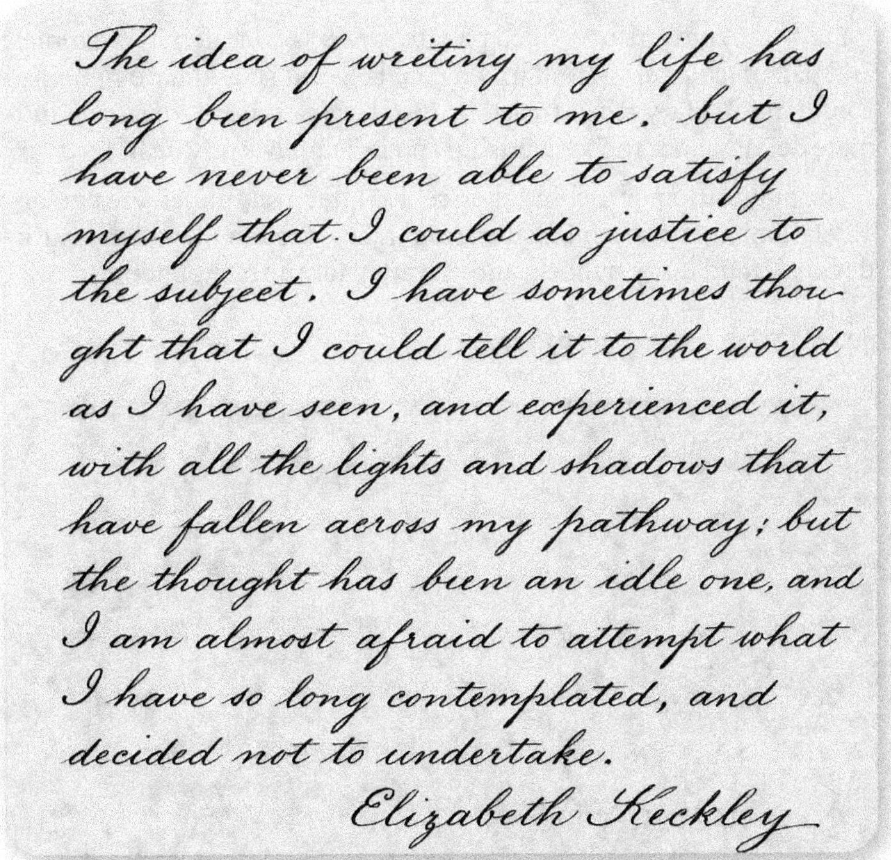

> The idea of writing my life has long been present to me, but I have never been able to satisfy myself that I could do justice to the subject. I have sometimes thought that I could tell it to the world as I have seen, and experienced it, with all the lights and shadows that have fallen across my pathway; but the thought has been an idle one, and I am almost afraid to attempt what I have so long contemplated, and decided not to undertake.
> — Elizabeth Keckley

Figure 108: A manuscript page from Elizabeth Keckley's memoir, showcasing her elegant handwriting and intellect.

The memoir was groundbreaking in several ways. It was one of the first published accounts of White House life written by someone who had been intimately involved in a presidential administration. It was also one of the first memoirs published by a formerly enslaved woman, providing perspectives on slavery and freedom that were rarely heard in public discourse.

Elizabeth's account of life in the Lincoln White House was detailed, respectful, and generally supportive of both Abraham and Mary Lincoln. She portrayed the president as a man of extraordinary character who was deeply committed to preserving the Union and ending slavery. She described Mary as a devoted wife and mother who was unfairly criticized for understandable behavior given the enormous pressures she faced.

But the memoir also revealed private conversations, family dynamics, and personal details that Mary Lincoln believed should have remained confidential. Mary felt betrayed by Elizabeth's decision to publish intimate details about their friendship and her family's private life.

The publication of "Behind the Scenes" effectively ended the personal relationship between Elizabeth and Mary, though Elizabeth continued to defend Mary publicly and privately for the rest of her life.

THE LEGACY OF INFLUENCE

Figure 109: Elizabeth Keckley teaching students at Wilberforce University in her later years.

Elizabeth Keckley lived until 1907, spending her final decades as a teacher and mentor to young black women who were seeking education and economic opportunities in the post-Civil War era. She established the Contraband Relief Association during the Civil War to provide assistance to formerly enslaved people who were flooding into Washington, and she continued this humanitarian work throughout her later life.

Despite the controversy it created, her memoir established Elizabeth as an important historical witness whose perspectives on slavery, emancipation, and the Lincoln presidency provided insights that were available nowhere else. Historians studying the Civil War and the Lincoln administration found her accounts to be remarkably accurate and valuable, even when they disagreed with her interpretations of events.

More importantly, Elizabeth's story demonstrated how individual relationships could influence major historical developments in ways that were largely invisible to the public. Her friendship with Mary Lincoln had provided stability and support that allowed the First Lady to function during the Civil War's most challenging moments. Her advice to both Abraham and Mary Lincoln had influenced policy decisions and political strategies that affected the entire nation.

Figure 110: The Lincoln Memorial with Keckley's memoir in the foreground, honoring her voice in

Elizabeth's role in the Lincoln White House also revealed how women, including women of color, could exercise significant political influence even when they were formally excluded from official power. She had shaped emancipation policy, military strategy, and political appointments through her relationships and access to key decision-makers.

This pattern of informal influence would be repeated throughout American history, as women found ways to affect political developments despite being denied formal political rights. Elizabeth Keckley's example showed that effective political influence often worked through personal relationships and behind-the-scenes advice rather than through official positions and public recognition.

THE UNACKNOWLEDGED ADVISOR

Figure 111: A composite portrait of Elizabeth Keckley and other overlooked women advisors who shaped American history.

Modern historians studying the Lincoln presidency have come to understand that Elizabeth Keckley was essentially an unofficial member of the Lincoln administration, providing advice and support that was crucial to the president's success. Her influence on policy development, particularly regarding emancipation and reconstruction, was more significant than that of many officially appointed advisors.

But Elizabeth's contributions were never formally acknowledged during her lifetime, and her role in the Lincoln presidency was largely forgotten after her death. This historical invisibility reflected the broader pattern of excluding women, and particularly women of color, from official recognition, even when they made significant contributions to American political development.

The rediscovery of Elizabeth Keckley's importance has been part of a broader historical reassessment that has revealed how many crucial contributions to American democracy were made by people who were formally excluded from political power. Women, minorities, immigrants, and other marginalized groups often influenced political developments through informal channels that left little trace in official records.

Figure 112: Researchers examining archival documents, uncovering hidden stories like Elizabeth Keckley's.

Elizabeth's story also illustrates how individual relationships and personal connections have always been crucial elements in American political development. The friendship between a formerly enslaved dressmaker and the First Lady created opportunities for influence and communication that wouldn't have existed through formal governmental channels.

This informal approach to political influence required extraordinary personal qualities, intelligence, discretion, empathy, and strategic thinking, which Elizabeth possessed in exceptional measure. Her success in navigating wartime Washington's complex social and political environment demonstrated capabilities that her society claimed formerly enslaved people couldn't develop.

THE WOMAN WHO HELPED HEAL A NATION

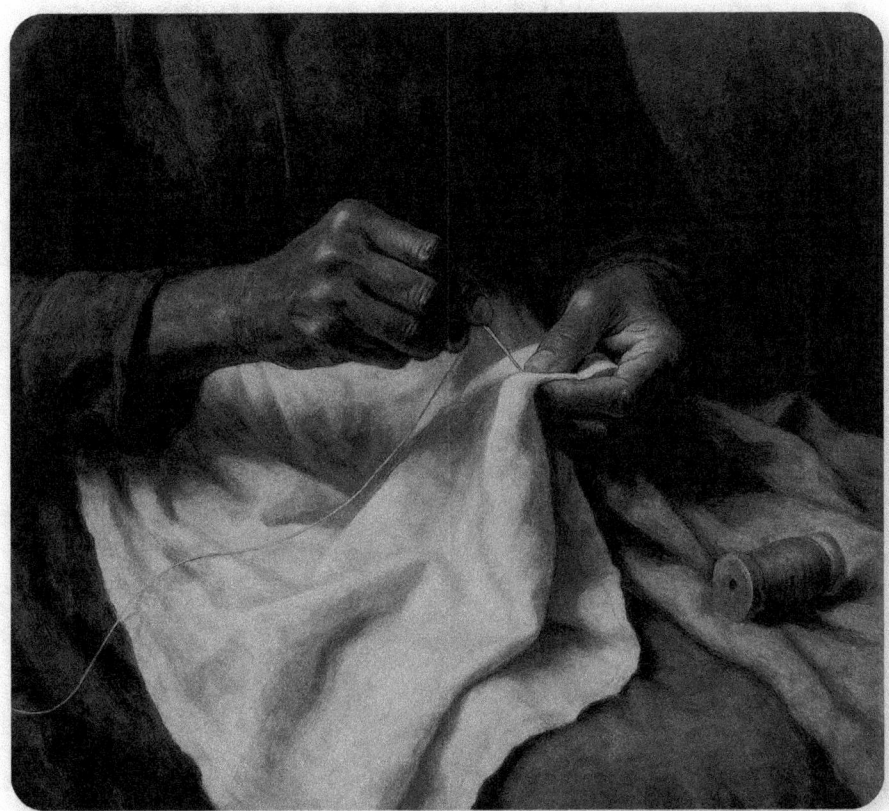

Figure 113: Elizabeth Keckley's hands stitching fabric, symbolizing her legacy in both fashion and history.

Elizabeth Keckley's greatest achievement wasn't creating elegant gowns for Washington's social elite or even providing crucial support to the Lincoln family during the Civil War. Her greatest achievement was demonstrating that formerly enslaved people could serve as advisors, confidantes, and informal leaders in the highest levels of American government.

Her relationship with Mary Lincoln proved that meaningful friendships could develop across racial lines even in a society that was built on racial hierarchy and separation. Her influence on Lincoln administration policy showed that formerly enslaved people could contribute to governmental decision-making in ways that benefited the entire nation.

Most importantly, Elizabeth's story illustrated how individual courage and competence could challenge systemic prejudices and create new possibilities for social progress. She hadn't set out to become a political influencer or a civil rights pioneer; she had simply focused on developing her skills, serving her clients, and supporting her friends. But her excellence in these roles created opportunities for broader influence that helped advance the cause of racial equality.

Figure 114: A modern sewing studio, echoing Elizabeth Keckley's lasting legacy in fashion and entrepreneurship

Elizabeth Keckley's journey from slave cabin to White House demonstrated that American democracy could be strengthened by including voices and perspectives that had previously been excluded from political discourse. Her advice to the Lincoln administration was valuable precisely because it came from someone who had experienced slavery firsthand and understood its effects on both black and white Americans.

Her example suggested that American society would be more effective and more just if it recognized and utilized the talents of all its people, regardless of their race, gender, or social background. The woman who dressed Mary Lincoln had also helped dress the wounds of a nation that was slowly and painfully learning how to live up to its founding ideals.

Elizabeth Keckley never held elected office or received official recognition for her contributions to American government. But she helped shape one of the most important presidencies in American history while demonstrating that the people who serve their country most effectively are often those who work quietly behind the scenes, building relationships and providing support that makes official leadership possible.

In the end, Elizabeth Keckley was more than Lincoln's other right hand. She was living proof that American democracy was strong enough to include everyone who was willing to contribute to its success.

Elizabeth Keckley's story reminds us that American history has always been shaped by informal advisors and behind-the-scenes influencers whose contributions remain largely hidden from public view. Her journey from slavery to the White House illustrates both the possibilities for individual achievement and the importance of recognizing how marginalized voices have always contributed to American political development. Her friendship with Mary Lincoln proved that meaningful relationships could transcend racial barriers even in America's most divided era. At the same time, her influence on Lincoln administration policy demonstrated that formerly enslaved people possessed wisdom and insights that could benefit the entire nation. Elizabeth Keckley never sought the spotlight, but her quiet strength helped hold together a presidency and a country during its darkest hours.

Chapter 7:
The Man Who Organized a Dream

BAYARD RUSTIN'S MARCH FOR JUSTICE

Figure 115: While an entire crowd celebrates his achievement, the man who made it possible remains in the shadows, a testament to his hidden heroism.

On the morning of August 28, 1963, as a quarter of a million Americans gathered at the Lincoln Memorial for the March on Washington for Jobs and Freedom, one man moved frantically through the crowds with clipboards, walkie-talkies, and an expression of barely controlled anxiety. While the world focused on the speakers who would soon make history, Bayard Rustin was worrying about portable toilets.

He had spent two months calculating how many restrooms would be needed for the largest political demonstration in American history. He had coordinated buses from across the country, arranged for first aid stations, and negotiated with police departments. He planned the precise timing that would allow dozens of speakers to deliver their messages without the crowd becoming restless or dispersed.

He had even arranged for the sound system that would carry Martin Luther King Jr.'s "I Have a Dream" speech to every corner of the National Mall, and to television audiences around the world.

But Bayard Rustin's name appeared nowhere on the official program. He gave no speeches, granted no interviews, and received no public recognition for organizing what many historians consider the most important political demonstration of the 20th century.

The reason was simple: Bayard Rustin was gay in an era when homosexuality could destroy careers, undermine movements, and provide ammunition for enemies who wanted to discredit the civil rights cause. The man who possessed the organizational genius to coordinate the March on Washington had to hide in the shadows because his sexuality made him a political liability.

Figure 116: History, as told by the media, often overlooks the unsung heroes who work behind the scenes.

Rustin's invisibility on that historic day was both a personal tragedy and a strategic necessity. His brilliance as an organizer had made the march possible, but his vulnerability as a gay man in 1960s America meant that he couldn't take credit for his achievement without risking the success of the movement he had devoted his life to serving.

The march succeeded beyond anyone's dreams, helping to build momentum for the Civil Rights Act of 1964 and the Voting Rights Act of 1965. But Bayard Rustin paid for that success with his own erasure from the history he had helped to make.

THE MAKING OF AN ORGANIZER

Figure 117: The intellectual fire and confidence of a young Bayard Rustin laid the groundwork for his future as a revolutionary organizer

Bayard Taylor Rustin was born in 1912 in West Chester, Pennsylvania, into a family that defied easy categorization in America's rigidly segregated society. His grandmother, Julia Davis Rustin, was a Quaker who believed that racial equality was a religious imperative rather than a political preference. She raised Bayard with the conviction that fighting injustice was not just morally right but spiritually necessary.

The Quaker influence on Rustin's development was profound and lasting. Quakers had been among the earliest opponents of slavery in America, and their commitment to nonviolence and social justice provided a framework for understanding how moral principles could be translated into political action. Young Bayard learned that true faith required working to create a more just society, not just believing in abstract principles.

But Rustin's family also provided him with something equally valuable: an example of how to maintain dignity and effectiveness while living as an outsider in American society. As black Quakers in a predominantly white religious community, and as prosperous blacks in a racially hostile environment, the Rustin family had learned to navigate complex social dynamics while never compromising their core values.

Figure 118: A young Bayard Rustin, already sharp and self-assured, forging the intellect that would shape movements.

Rustin's intellectual gifts became apparent early. He excelled in school, demonstrated exceptional musical ability, and showed a natural talent for public speaking and debate. But he also displayed the personal characteristics that would make him both an extraordinary organizer and a perpetual outsider: he was uncompromisingly honest about his beliefs, fearlessly willing to challenge authority, and completely uninterested in conforming to social expectations that he considered unjust.

By the time Rustin reached college, he had already begun integrating his Quaker commitment to nonviolence with his growing understanding of systematic racial oppression. He was particularly influenced by Mahatma Gandhi's successful use of nonviolent resistance against British colonial rule in India, seeing parallels between Indian independence struggles and American civil rights challenges.

But Rustin's college years also brought him face-to-face with the reality that would define his entire adult life: he was homosexual in a society that considered homosexuality both criminal and sinful. This discovery forced him to develop strategies for managing a secret that could destroy his effectiveness as a civil rights organizer while never allowing that secret to diminish his commitment to justice for others.

The young man who would later organize the March on Washington learned early that personal authenticity and political effectiveness sometimes required impossible choices. Bayard Rustin chose effectiveness over authenticity, devoting his life to advancing civil rights while hiding the part of his identity that could undermine that work.

THE STRATEGIST IN THE SHADOWS

Figure 119: The methodical work behind the scenes, often out of the spotlight, is what makes great movements possible.

By the 1940s, Bayard Rustin had become one of America's most sophisticated theorists and practitioners of nonviolent resistance. He had studied Gandhi's methods intensively, traveled to India to learn directly from veterans of the independence movement, and developed strategies for applying nonviolent principles to American racial conflicts.

Rustin's approach to civil rights organizing was revolutionary in its combination of moral conviction and tactical sophistication. He understood that successful movements required more than righteous anger; they needed careful planning, strategic thinking, and meticulous attention to logistics that would allow protesters to maintain nonviolent discipline even under extreme provocation.

His first major success came with the Journey of Reconciliation in 1947, a precursor to the more famous Freedom Rides of the 1960s. Rustin organized a series of bus trips through the upper South to test compliance with Supreme Court decisions that had declared segregated interstate travel unconstitutional.

Figure 120: The quiet and determined early work of Bayard Rustin, captured in this 1947 Journey of Reconciliation photograph, laid the foundation for his future as a civil rights leader.

The Journey of Reconciliation demonstrated Rustin's genius for combining moral witness with practical strategy. He understood that nonviolent resistance was most effective when it exposed the violence that was inherent in segregation systems, forcing white Americans to confront the brutality that maintained racial hierarchy.

But the Journey of Reconciliation also revealed the personal costs of Rustin's commitment to civil rights work. He was arrested multiple times during the bus trips. He spent several weeks on a North Carolina chain gang, experiencing firsthand the violence and degradation that the segregation system used to maintain white supremacy.

More importantly for his future role in the movement, the Journey of Reconciliation established Rustin's reputation as someone who could organize complex, multi-state operations that required coordination between different organizations, careful legal preparation, and extensive media planning.

By the 1950s, Rustin had become the person that other civil rights leaders called when they needed strategic advice about organizing large-scale demonstrations, coordinating media coverage, or developing nonviolent tactics that would be effective against specific forms of segregation.

THE MENTOR BEHIND THE ICON

Figure 121: King and Rustin in deep dialogue—where vision met strategy in the fight for civil rights."

When a young minister named Martin Luther King Jr. emerged as a leader during the Montgomery Bus Boycott in 1955, he had moral authority and inspiring rhetoric but little experience with the practical challenges of organizing sustained resistance movements. Recognizing King's potential, Bayard Rustin quietly traveled to Montgomery to offer strategic advice and organizational support.

Rustin's contribution to the Montgomery Bus Boycott was enormous but largely invisible. He helped King develop the philosophical framework that would become known as the Montgomery method, combining Christian theology with Gandhian nonviolence in ways that could inspire mass participation while maintaining movement discipline.

More importantly, Rustin helped King understand the practical requirements for sustaining a year-long economic boycott that would require alternative transportation systems, financial coordination, and careful media management that would build national support for the Montgomery protesters.

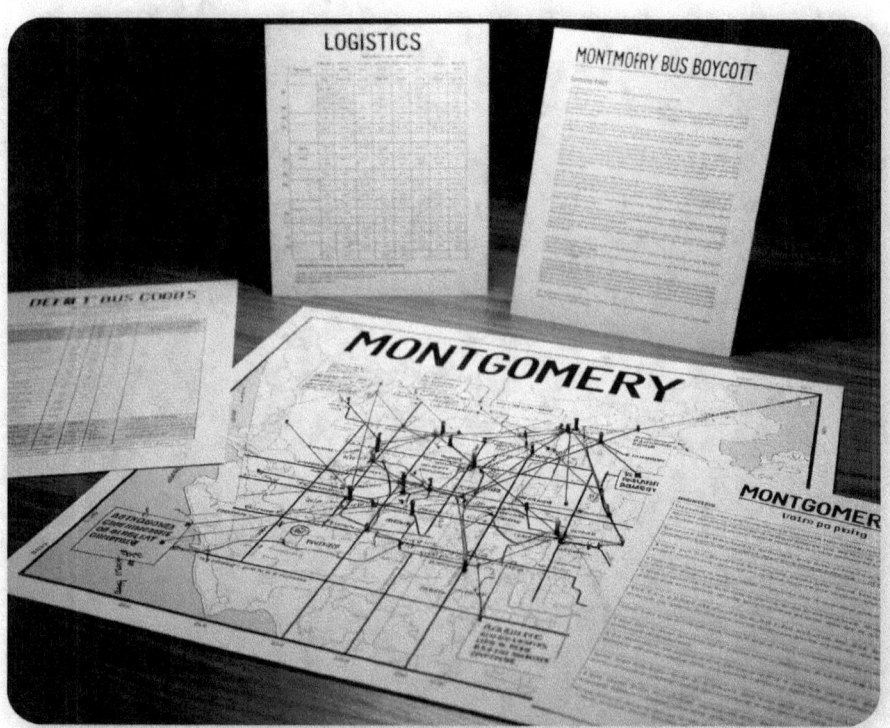

Figure 122: The careful logistics of the Montgomery Bus Boycott show that even a movement of the people requires meticulous planning.

The relationship between Rustin and King during this period was complex and sometimes tense. King recognized Rustin's invaluable strategic insights but was increasingly concerned about the political risks of being closely associated with someone whose homosexuality could provide ammunition for movement opponents.

These concerns intensified as King's national profile grew and conservative critics began looking for ways to discredit the civil rights movement. FBI director J. Edgar Hoover was already investigating King's associates for communist connections, and King's advisors worried that Rustin's homosexuality could provide additional grounds for attacking the movement's legitimacy.

The result was a pattern that would define Rustin's relationship with the civil rights movement for the rest of his career: he would provide crucial strategic advice and organizational support while remaining largely invisible to the public, protecting both his own effectiveness and the movement's reputation.

This arrangement was personally painful for Rustin, who possessed the intellectual and oratorical gifts that could have made him a powerful public spokesperson for civil rights. But he accepted his behind-the-scenes role because he understood that his personal visibility could damage the cause that mattered more than his individual recognition.

THE SECRET ARCHITECT

Figure 123 The planning documents for the March on Washington show the extraordinary detail and coordination required for a successful mass demonstration.

When civil rights leaders began discussing the possibility of a massive demonstration in Washington, D.C. in early 1963, they faced organizational challenges that seemed almost impossible to overcome. How do you coordinate transportation for hundreds of thousands of people from across the country? How do you provide food, water, and sanitation for a crowd larger than the population of most American cities? How do you maintain order and discipline among demonstrators who would include everyone from conservative church members to radical activists?

Most importantly, how do you organize a demonstration large enough to influence congressional action on civil rights legislation, while ensuring that the event remains peaceful and doesn't provide ammunition for opponents who claimed that civil rights activists were dangerous radicals?

The answer was Bayard Rustin, whose two decades of experience with nonviolent organizing had given him the skills needed to coordinate the most complex political demonstration in American history.

Figure 124: The tireless work of unsung heroes, like Bayard Rustin, is often conducted in the chaos of a busy office, where every detail matters.

Rustin's appointment as chief organizer for the March on Washington was controversial within the civil rights leadership. Many leaders, including some who respected his abilities, worried that his homosexuality made him too vulnerable to enemy attacks. Others questioned whether someone who had never held a major leadership position in civil rights organizations should be trusted with such a crucial responsibility.

But A. Philip Randolph, the veteran labor leader who had originally proposed the march idea, insisted that Rustin was the only person in America who possessed the organizational skills needed to make the demonstration successful. Randolph had worked with Rustin for years and understood that his strategic genius was essential to the march's success.

The compromise that emerged reflected both Rustin's indispensability and his vulnerability: he would serve as chief organizer but would have no official title and would receive no public recognition. His work would be crucial but invisible, protecting both the march and the movement from attacks based on his sexuality.

Rustin accepted this arrangement without complaint, understanding that the march's success mattered more than his personal recognition. He had spent his entire career working behind the scenes for civil rights, and he was willing to make that sacrifice one more time for what might be the movement's most important demonstration.

THE IMPOSSIBLE LOGISTICS

Figure 125: The transportation coordination for the march was a logistical marvel, bringing people together from all corners of the country.

Organizing the March on Washington required Bayard Rustin to solve logistical problems that had never been attempted in American political history. In just eight weeks, he had to coordinate transportation, housing, food, security, and media coverage for an event that could include anywhere from 100,000 to 500,000 participants.

The transportation challenge alone was staggering. Rustin had to coordinate with bus companies, train operators, and airline carriers to move demonstrators from every state in the country to Washington, D.C. on a single day. He had to negotiate special rates, plan routes that would avoid traffic congestion, and coordinate arrival times that would allow the demonstration to begin on schedule.

But transportation was just the beginning. Rustin also had to arrange for portable toilets (his calculations suggested that 292 portable restrooms would be needed for a crowd of 100,000 people), first aid stations, water fountains, and food vendors that could serve the massive crowd without creating chaos or unsanitary conditions.

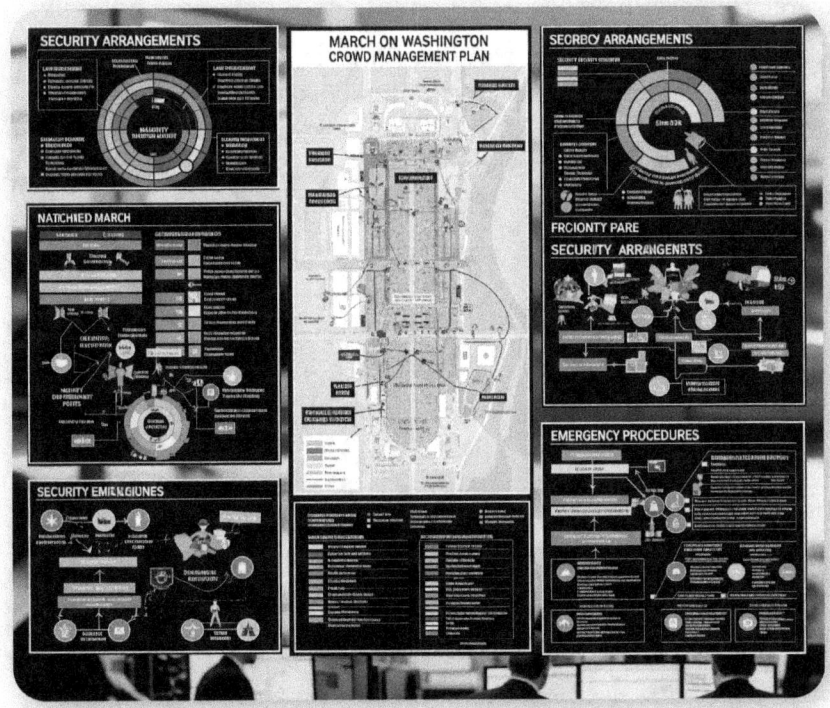

Figure 126: This meticulous planning was the unseen backbone of the March on Washington, ensuring the safety and success of the historic event.

Most importantly, Rustin had to develop security and crowd control procedures that would prevent violence while allowing for peaceful demonstrations. He worked closely with Washington D.C. police and federal law enforcement agencies to create protocols that would protect demonstrators from hostile counter-protesters while ensuring that the march itself remained completely nonviolent.

Rustin's approach to these challenges revealed his genius for combining idealistic goals with practical problem-solving. He understood that the march would succeed or fail based on mundane details like bathroom facilities and traffic flow, not just on the inspiring speeches that would capture media attention.

His planning documents from this period read like military operation orders, with detailed timelines, contingency plans, and backup procedures for every demonstration aspect. He had learned from decades of organizing experience that successful movements required meticulous attention to practical details that less experienced organizers often overlooked.

The result was an organizational achievement that impressed even the march's critics. Conservative politicians who opposed civil rights legislation acknowledged that the demonstration was extraordinarily well-organized and disciplined, making it difficult to dismiss the marchers as dangerous radicals or unruly protesters.

THE DAY THAT CHANGED AMERICA

Figure 127: The visual impact of this massive crowd is a testament to the organizational achievement of Bayard Rustin.

On the morning of August 28, 1963, Bayard Rustin's eight weeks of intensive planning culminated in what many historians consider the most successful political demonstration in American history. More than 250,000 Americans gathered peacefully at the Lincoln Memorial to demand congressional action on civil rights legislation and bear witness to racial equality's moral urgency.

The march exceeded every expectation for size, diversity, and impact. The crowd included not just civil rights activists but labor union members, religious leaders, college students, and middle-class families who had never participated in political demonstrations before. The racial composition was approximately 75% black and 25% white, demonstrating the interracial coalition that civil rights leaders had been trying to build for decades.

Most importantly, the march's disciplined nonviolence and dignified atmosphere made it impossible for opponents to dismiss the demonstrators as dangerous extremists. The peaceful, orderly nature of the event actually strengthened arguments for civil rights legislation by demonstrating that responsible citizens, rather than radical agitators, led the movement.

Figure 128: King speaks a dream to the world—powered by Rustin's vision behind the scenes

For Bayard Rustin, watching the march unfold was simultaneously the greatest triumph and the most painful moment of his career. His organizational genius had made possible a demonstration that would influence American politics for generations. His meticulous planning had ensured that every detail worked perfectly, from the sound system that carried speeches to the back of the crowd to the transportation that got demonstrators home safely that evening.

But Rustin experienced this triumph as an invisible participant, watching from the sidelines as other leaders received credit for an achievement that was largely his creation. He could not give interviews, make speeches, or even stand prominently on the platform during the formal program.

The march's success validated everything Rustin had believed about the power of nonviolent organization and strategic planning. But his invisibility during the event also confirmed the personal costs of his commitment to civil rights work in a society that was not ready to accept gay leaders in any context.

THE PRICE OF INVISIBILITY

Figure 129: Newspaper headlines often tell a simplified story, leaving out the hidden heroes who make the events possible.

In the weeks following the March on Washington, as media coverage celebrated the demonstration's success and political observers assessed its impact on civil rights legislation, Bayard Rustin's role in organizing the event was largely ignored or minimized.

Civil rights leaders who knew the truth about Rustin's contributions faced a difficult dilemma. They wanted to acknowledge his crucial role in making the march successful. Still, they also understood that highlighting his contributions could provide ammunition for opponents who were already trying to discredit the civil rights movement.

Conservative politicians and segregationist newspapers were actively looking for ways to undermine the march's positive impact, and many movement leaders worried that revealing Rustin's central role would give enemies the opportunity to shift public discussion from civil rights issues to questions about the sexual orientation of movement organizers.

Figure 130: While law enforcement was watching, the seeds of change were being planted in plain sight.

The Federal Bureau of Investigation, under J. Edgar Hoover's direction, was already conducting extensive surveillance of civil rights leaders and looking for evidence that could be used to discredit the movement. FBI files from this period show that Hoover's agents were particularly interested in finding evidence of communist connections or personal scandals that could be used against prominent civil rights figures.

Rustin's homosexuality made him especially vulnerable to this kind of attack, since sexual nonconformity was widely viewed as evidence of moral weakness or security risk during the Cold War era. Movement leaders understood that protecting Rustin's secret was essential not just for his personal safety but for the movement's political effectiveness.

The result was a conspiracy of silence that protected both Rustin and the movement but also ensured that one of the most important organizers in civil rights history would remain largely unknown to the American public.

This silence was personally devastating for Rustin, who had devoted his entire adult life to advancing civil rights while being forced to hide a crucial part of his identity. He had accepted the necessity of staying in the shadows, but the complete erasure of his contributions to the march was more painful than he had anticipated.

THE CONTINUING STRUGGLE

Figure 131: Bayard Rustin, still teaching truth, long after the spotlight faded.

After the March on Washington, Bayard Rustin continued working for civil rights and social justice. Still, his influence within the mainstream movement gradually diminished as younger, more radical activists questioned both his commitment to nonviolence and his willingness to work within existing political systems.

The rise of Black Power movements in the late 1960s created additional challenges for Rustin, whose integrationist philosophy and commitment to interracial coalitions seemed increasingly outdated to activists who emphasized black nationalism and separatism. His homosexuality, which had made him vulnerable to conservative attacks, also made him suspect among Black Power advocates who viewed sexual nonconformity as incompatible with black masculinity.

Rustin responded to these challenges by expanding his focus beyond civil rights to include broader economic justice issues, international human rights, and democratic socialism. He became an advocate for labor rights, gay rights, and refugee assistance, applying the organizational skills he had developed in civil rights work to other social justice causes.

Figure 132: he continued activism of Bayard Rustin with labor and human rights organizations, showcasing his commitment to justice beyond civil rights.

But Rustin's marginalization within the civil rights movement meant that his later work received little attention from mainstream media or political leaders. The man who had organized the March on Washington was increasingly viewed as a relic from an earlier, more moderate phase of civil rights activism.

This marginalization was particularly painful because it coincided with growing public acceptance of gay rights activism. By the 1970s, a visible gay rights movement was beginning to challenge legal and social discrimination against homosexuals. Still, Rustin was too identified with civil rights organizations that were uncomfortable with gay issues to become a prominent figure in this new movement.

The result was that Rustin remained caught between two worlds: civil rights organizations that valued his contributions but were uncomfortable with his sexuality, and gay rights organizations that respected his identity but were unfamiliar with his achievements in civil rights work.

THE DELAYED RECOGNITION

Figure 133: Late in life, Bayard Rustin receives long-overdue recognition for a lifetime of unseen leadership

Bayard Rustin began receiving appropriate recognition for his contributions to civil rights only in the final decades of his life, as historians gained access to previously classified documents and as social attitudes toward homosexuality began to change.

The first major reassessment of Rustin's role came from academic historians who were studying the internal dynamics of civil rights organizations and discovered the extent of his influence on movement strategy and tactics. Scholars who interviewed other civil rights leaders learned that Rustin had been the primary architect of many successful campaigns that had been publicly credited to other organizers.

The release of FBI surveillance files through Freedom of Information Act requests also revealed the extent to which federal law enforcement had recognized Rustin's importance, even when civil rights organizations were keeping his role secret. Despite his lack of public prominence, the FBI documents showed that Hoover's agents considered Rustin one of the most dangerous and effective civil rights organizers.

Figure 134: The unseen hero's importance is often first recognized in the confidential files of those who fear his influence.

More importantly, changing social attitudes toward homosexuality made it possible for civil rights organizations to acknowledge Rustin's contributions without fearing political backlash. By the 1980s, gay rights had become a legitimate political cause supported by many of the same liberal coalitions that had backed civil rights legislation.

Rustin himself began speaking more openly about his experiences as a gay man in the civil rights movement. However, he never expressed bitterness about the movement's earlier reluctance to acknowledge his sexuality. He understood that social change required compromise and strategic thinking, and he remained committed to the movements that had shaped his life even when they had forced him to remain invisible.

When Rustin died in 1987, his obituaries finally provided full recognition of his contributions to civil rights and social justice. The man who had organized the March on Washington was finally acknowledged as one of the most important strategists in the history of American social movements.

THE POSTHUMOUS LEGACY

Figure 135: The modern gay rights march shows how the legacy of Bayard Rustin continues to inspire new generations of activists.

Since Bayard Rustin's death, his legacy has been embraced by both civil rights organizations and gay rights activists who recognize him as a pioneering figure who advanced both causes despite the personal costs of living at their intersection.

Civil rights organizations that once kept Rustin in the shadows now celebrate him as a founding strategist whose organizational genius was essential to the movement's success. The March on Washington is now commonly described as "Bayard Rustin's march," acknowledging his central role in its planning and execution.

Gay rights organizations have claimed Rustin as a pioneering figure who demonstrated that sexual minorities could make crucial contributions to social justice movements even when they were forced to hide their identities. His example has inspired LGBTQ+ activists who work within other social movements while advocating for recognition and inclusion.

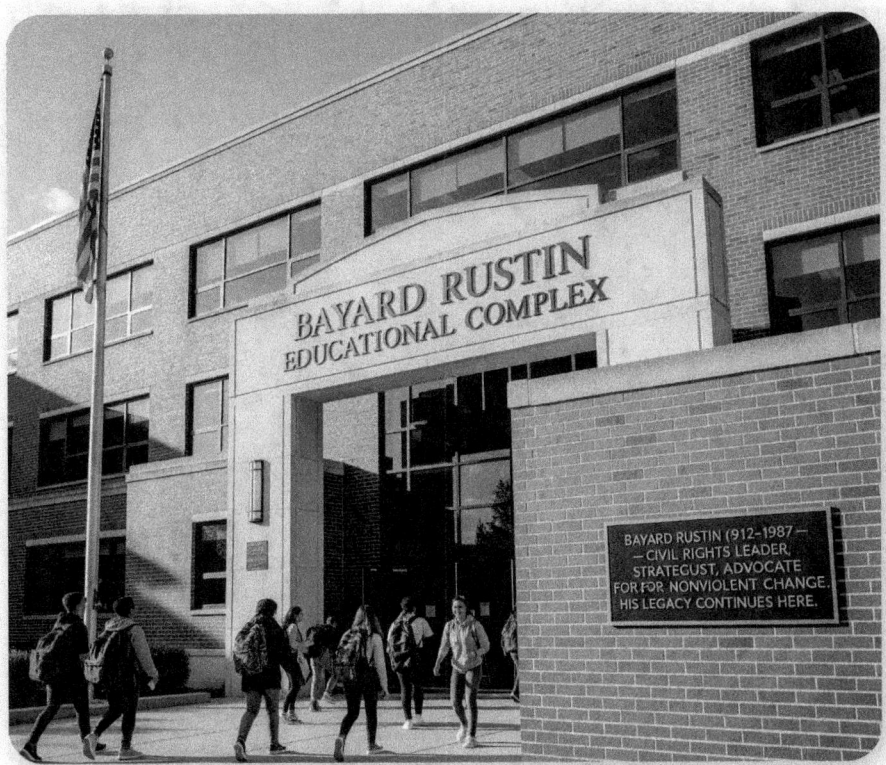

Figure 136: An institution named in his honor ensures that Bayard Rustin's legacy and contributions are officially recognized and celebrated.

Educational institutions, civil rights organizations, and government agencies now honor Rustin's memory through scholarships, awards, and facilities that bear his name. In 2013, President Barack Obama awarded Rustin a posthumous Presidential Medal of Freedom, the nation's highest civilian honor, acknowledging contributions that had been ignored for decades.

But perhaps Rustin's most important legacy is the example he provided of how individuals can serve causes larger than themselves, even when those causes cannot fully acknowledge their contributions. His willingness to sacrifice personal recognition for movement success demonstrated a form of selfless and strategic leadership.

THE ORGANIZER'S TRUE VICTORY

Figure 137: The enduring influence of Bayard Rustin's organizational methods continues to shape modern activism.

Bayard Rustin's greatest achievement wasn't organizing the March on Washington, though that demonstration changed American politics and inspired social justice movements around the world. His greatest achievement was proving that effective organizing could create possibilities for social change that seemed impossible when the work began.

When Rustin started his career as a civil rights organizer in the 1940s, racial segregation was legally enforced throughout the South and socially accepted throughout most of the North. The idea that a quarter of a million Americans would gather peacefully in the nation's capital to demand racial equality would have seemed like a fantasy to most observers.

But Rustin understood that social change required more than moral arguments or inspiring speeches. It required patient organizing, strategic planning, and careful attention to the practical details that would allow movements to sustain themselves over time and achieve concrete political victories.

Figure 138: The influence of Rustin's organizing methods is clearly seen in the detailed, strategic planning of today's young activists.

His methods of nonviolent organizing, coalition building, and strategic planning became templates that social justice movements around the world have used. Environmental activists, immigrant rights organizers, and economic justice advocates have all adapted techniques that Rustin pioneered during his decades of civil rights work.

More importantly, Rustin's example demonstrated that social change is possible when people are willing to work for causes larger than their own immediate interests. His sacrifice of personal recognition for movement success showed that true leadership often requires accepting invisibility to serve larger goals.

The man who organized a dream proved that dreams can become reality when they are supported by meticulous planning, strategic thinking, and the willingness to do whatever work is necessary to make change possible.

Bayard Rustin may have been forced to hide in the shadows during the March on Washington, but his light continues illuminating the path toward a more just society. His legacy reminds us that the people who change the world are often those who never seek credit for their achievements, but who pour their talents into causes that will outlive their individual contributions.

Bayard Rustin's story illustrates the complex relationship between personal identity and public service in American social movements. His genius as an organizer helped create some of the most important moments in civil rights history, but his sexuality forced him to remain largely invisible during his lifetime. His example reminds us that social progress often depends on individuals who are willing to sacrifice personal recognition for collective advancement, and that the people who do the most important work are often those who receive the least recognition. Rustin's legacy challenges us to look beyond the famous faces and inspiring speeches to recognize the behind-the-scenes organizers whose strategic thinking and tireless work make social change possible. His life demonstrates that true leadership sometimes requires accepting invisibility and that people who never get to take credit for their achievements often achieve the greatest victories.

Chapter 8:
The Mother of a Movement

ELLA BAKER: THE WOMAN WHO TAUGHT LEADERS HOW TO LEAD

Figure 139: In this small room, the seeds of change are planted not by celebrity leaders, but through the patient, powerful work of grassroots organizers.

In April 1960, as college students across the South launched sit-in protests that would transform the civil rights movement, a fifty-seven-year-old woman named Ella Baker did something that would have been unthinkable to most adults of her generation: she listened to teenagers tell her how they planned to change the world.

Baker had called a meeting at Shaw University in Raleigh, North Carolina, to bring together student activists who had been organizing lunch counter protests across the South. Older civil rights leaders expected the meeting to produce a youth auxiliary that would support existing organizations and follow strategies developed by experienced adults.

Instead, Baker encouraged the students to form their own independent organization with their own strategies and their own leadership structure. She believed that meaningful social change had to come from the people most affected by injustice, not from charismatic leaders or established organizations telling those people what to do.

"Remember," she told the young activists, "the movement made Martin, not Martin the movement."

Figure 140: The founding meeting of SNCC brought together young, passionate voices, ready to lead the charge for nonviolent change.

That meeting led to the formation of the Student Nonviolent Coordinating Committee (SNCC), which would become the most dynamic and influential organization of the civil rights era. SNCC's young activists would organize Freedom Rides, voter registration drives, and community organizing projects that reached into the deepest corners of the segregated South.

But the person who made SNCC possible, who nurtured its development, provided strategic guidance, and protected its independence, was Ella Baker, whose philosophy of grassroots organizing and participatory democracy challenged everything that Americans thought they knew about leadership and social change.

Baker believed that real power came from ordinary people working together to solve their own problems, not from inspiring speeches or charismatic personalities. She thought that effective movements built lasting change by developing the leadership capacity of entire communities, not by depending on a few exceptional individuals.

Most importantly, she was convinced that democracy worked best when it included the voices and perspectives of people who had been traditionally excluded from decision-making processes, especially women, young people, and poor people who lived in the communities most affected by injustice.

These ideas made Ella Baker one of the most influential strategists in civil rights history. They also made her one of the most overlooked, because her approach to organizing was designed to make other people famous rather than building her own public profile.

THE MAKING OF A REVOLUTIONARY

Figure 141: The intellectual and political foundations of Ella Baker were formed in the vibrant academic environment of Shaw University.

Ella Jo Baker was born in 1903 in Norfolk, Virginia, to parents who understood that education was the key to advancement in a society that offered few opportunities for black achievement. Her mother, Georgianna Ross Baker, was a former teacher who had sacrificed her own career to raise her children. However, she was determined that they would have opportunities she had been denied.

Baker's family moved to North Carolina when she was young, settling in a rural community where her grandmother told stories about slavery and Reconstruction that shaped Baker's understanding of how social change happened. Her grandmother had lived through emancipation and had seen how formerly enslaved people had organized schools, churches, and political organizations to advance their own interests rather than waiting for white authorities to grant them rights.

These stories taught Baker that ordinary people possessed the wisdom and capability to improve their own conditions when they were given opportunities to work together. She learned that sustainable social change came from community organizing and collective action, not from depending on exceptional leaders or outside assistance.

Figure 142: The roots of community organizing and collective action run deep, shaping the future of civil rights.

At Shaw University, Baker excelled academically while developing the intellectual framework that would guide her lifelong commitment to social justice. She studied sociology and political science but was more influenced by her observations of how students organized themselves to address campus issues and community problems.

Baker noticed that the most effective student activism happened when students identified their priorities and developed strategies, rather than following directives from faculty or administration. She saw that young people often had insights about social problems that older, more established leaders missed, and that their energy and creativity could generate innovative approaches to persistent challenges.

Most importantly, Baker learned that effective organizing required patient relationship-building rather than dramatic public events. The students who created lasting change were those who spent time listening to their peers, building trust across different social groups, and developing collective leadership structures that could survive graduation and personnel changes.

These observations about student organizing would later influence Baker's approach to civil rights work, as she applied lessons learned on college campuses to the challenges of organizing entire communities for social change.

THE NAACP YEARS

Figure 143: The tireless work of Ella Baker, traveling through the rural South, laid the groundwork for grassroots organizing.

After graduating from Shaw University in 1927, Ella Baker moved to New York City during the height of the Harlem Renaissance, planning to pursue graduate study and a career in social work. But the Great Depression changed her plans, as the economic crisis made graduate school unaffordable and forced her to focus on more immediate survival concerns.

Baker found work with various social service organizations in Harlem, where she learned about the practical challenges of organizing poor and working-class communities for political action. She discovered that effective community organizing required understanding the daily struggles that people faced, including unemployment, inadequate housing, poor schools, police brutality, and connecting those immediate concerns to larger questions about systemic change.

In 1940, Baker joined the National Association for the Advancement of Colored People (NAACP) as a field secretary, responsible for organizing new chapters throughout the South and helping existing chapters develop more effective advocacy strategies.

Figure 144: The quiet church where Ella Baker held meetings was the true birthplace of the civil rights movement's grassroots power.

Baker's approach to NAACP organizing was revolutionary within the organization's traditional framework. Instead of focusing primarily on legal strategies and lobbying efforts directed by the national office, she emphasized building strong local chapters that could address community-specific problems while supporting broader civil rights goals.

She spent months at a time traveling through the rural South, staying in people's homes, eating at their tables, and listening to their stories about how segregation affected their daily lives. She learned that national NAACP strategies often failed to address the most pressing concerns of local communities, and that sustainable organizing required developing leadership capacity within those communities rather than depending on direction from distant headquarters.

Most importantly, Baker discovered that the most effective local leaders were often women who had been excluded from formal leadership roles but who possessed extensive networks of relationships and a deep understanding of community needs. She began deliberately cultivating female leadership within NAACP chapters, recognizing that women's organizing skills and community knowledge were essential resources that the civil rights movement was systematically underutilizing.

This focus on developing grassroots leadership, particularly among women and young people, brought Baker into conflict with NAACP national leadership, which preferred centralized control and formal organizational structures. But it also made her chapters among the most effective and sustainable in the organization, as local leaders developed the skills and confidence needed to address their own communities' problems.

THE PHILOSOPHY OF PARTICIPATORY DEMOCRACY

Figure 145: A true leader's power is not in giving orders, but in fostering the voice of the community.

During her years with the NAACP, Ella Baker developed a philosophy of organizing that challenged fundamental assumptions about leadership, power, and social change that dominated American political culture. Her approach, which she called "participatory democracy," emphasized developing the leadership capacity of entire communities rather than depending on charismatic individuals or established institutions.

Baker believed that ordinary people possessed the wisdom and capability to solve their own problems when they were given opportunities to work together and access to information about political processes. She thought that meaningful democracy required genuine participation by all community members, especially those who had been traditionally excluded from decision-making because of their race, gender, class, or age.

Most controversially, Baker argued that movements led by charismatic personalities were ultimately less effective than movements that developed collective leadership structures. She worried that dependence on exceptional individuals made movements vulnerable to personality conflicts, government targeting, and the inevitable limitations of any single person's perspective or capabilities.

Figure 146: A community where all voices are heard is a community empowered to create change.

This philosophy put Baker at odds with the leadership style that was becoming dominant in civil rights organizations during the 1950s. As Martin Luther King Jr. emerged as the movement's most prominent spokesperson, other organizations began adopting similar models that emphasized charismatic leadership and media-focused strategies.

Baker respected King's abilities and supported his work. Still, she worried that the movement was becoming too dependent on his individual leadership and too focused on dramatic public events rather than sustained community organizing. She thought that lasting social change required building institutions and developing leaders at the grassroots level, not just winning legislative victories or generating favorable media coverage.

Her concerns proved prescient as the civil rights movement faced increasing challenges in the late 1960s. Organizations that had depended heavily on charismatic leadership struggled to maintain effectiveness when those leaders were assassinated, discredited, or simply exhausted by the demands of constant public attention.

Meanwhile, organizations like SNCC that had been built on Baker's model of collective leadership and grassroots organizing proved more resilient and adaptable to changing political circumstances.

THE MIDWIFE OF SNCC

Figure 147: In the spirit of Ella Baker's grassroots philosophy, these young activists are the catalysts for change, empowering communities from the ground up.

When college students began launching sit-in protests across the South in early 1960, established civil rights organizations saw an opportunity to recruit young activists into existing organizational structures. The NAACP, the Southern Christian Leadership Conference (SCLC), and other groups invited student leaders to meetings where they could be educated about proper protest strategies and integrated into adult-led organizations.

Ella Baker had a different idea. As SCLC's executive director, she was officially supposed to encourage the students to work within existing organizations and follow strategies developed by experienced leaders. Instead, she used SCLC resources to organize a meeting that would allow students to develop their own independent organization with their own priorities and strategies.

The Raleigh meeting in April 1960 was structured according to Baker's philosophy of participatory democracy. Instead of featuring speeches by prominent leaders, the meeting consisted primarily of small group discussions where students could share their experiences, identify common challenges, and develop collective strategies for future action.

Figure 148: n these small group discussions, the spirit of democratic organizing thrived, empowering young activists to lead their own movement.

Baker's role at the meeting was deliberately minimal but strategically crucial. She provided logistical support and facilitated discussions, but avoided giving speeches or trying to influence the students' decisions about organizational structure or strategic priorities. Her goal was to create space for young people to develop their own leadership rather than imposing adult perspectives on student activism.

The result was the formation of SNCC, an organization that embodied Baker's vision of democratic organizing and collective leadership. SNCC had no single leader or spokesperson but operated through consensus decision-making processes that ensured all members could participate in strategic planning.

More importantly, SNCC was committed to community organizing that developed local leadership capacity rather than depending on outside organizers or national media attention. SNCC activists would spend months or years living in communities, building relationships with local residents, and helping them develop their own organizations and strategies for addressing local problems.

This approach made SNCC the most effective grassroots organizing force in civil rights history. Still, it also made it difficult for mainstream media and political leaders to understand or control the organization.

THE FREEDOM SUMMER STRATEGY

Figure 149: In these grassroots efforts, the philosophy of Ella Baker came to life, empowering local communities to fight for their own rights.

SNCC's most ambitious organizing project came in 1964, when the organization decided to focus national attention on voting rights violations in Mississippi by bringing hundreds of white college students south to work on voter registration drives. The project, known as Freedom Summer, was designed according to Baker's principles of grassroots organizing and community empowerment.

Unlike other civil rights campaigns that focused on dramatic confrontations with segregationist authorities, Freedom Summer emphasized patient, sustained organizing that would build long-term capacity for political participation in black communities. SNCC organizers would work with local residents to establish Freedom Schools that provided education about voting rights and political processes, and to create parallel political institutions like the Mississippi Freedom Democratic Party that would challenge white-controlled political structures.

Baker's influence on Freedom Summer strategy was profound but largely invisible. She didn't travel to Mississippi or receive media attention for the project, but her organizing philosophy shaped every aspect of SNCC's approach to the campaign.

Figure 150: The Freedom Schools were a testament to the power of education as a tool for organizing, building knowledge and community from the ground up.

Most importantly, Baker's emphasis on developing local leadership meant that Freedom Summer was designed to strengthen existing black communities rather than creating dependence on outside organizers. SNCC volunteers were trained to support local initiatives and help residents develop their own leadership skills, rather than imposing outside strategies or taking over local organizations.

This approach made Freedom Summer more sustainable and effective than campaigns that depended on temporary media attention or federal intervention. The relationships and institutions that SNCC organizers helped build during Freedom Summer continued to influence Mississippi politics for decades after the volunteers returned to their home communities.

But Baker's organizing philosophy also made Freedom Summer more dangerous and controversial than other civil rights campaigns. By focusing on voter registration and political organizing rather than symbolic protests, SNCC was directly challenging the economic and political power structures that maintained white supremacy in Mississippi.

The result was massive violent retaliation, including the murders of three civil rights workers and countless attacks on local residents who supported voter registration efforts. But the violence also exposed the brutality of segregation in ways that generated national support for voting rights legislation.

THE FEMINIST PIONEER

Figure 151: The powerful female networks behind the civil rights movement, often operating outside of the public eye, were essential to its success.

Throughout her civil rights career, Ella Baker challenged not only racial segregation but also the gender hierarchies that limited women's leadership roles within civil rights organizations. Her approach to organizing deliberately created space for women's voices and perspectives, recognizing that female community leaders possessed knowledge and skills that were essential to movement success.

Baker noticed that civil rights organizations typically excluded women from formal leadership positions while depending heavily on women's volunteer labor for fundraising, communication, and community outreach. She saw that this pattern wasted enormous human resources while reinforcing sexist assumptions about women's capabilities and appropriate roles.

Her response was to develop organizing strategies, highlighting women's leadership and creating opportunities for female activists to exercise real decision-making power. In NAACP chapters, SCLC campaigns, and SNCC projects, Baker consistently promoted women to positions of responsibility and encouraged them to develop their own political analysis and strategic thinking.

Figure 152: The power of a movement is in the hands of its organizers.

This feminist approach to organizing was controversial within civil rights organizations that were dominated by male ministers and lawyers who viewed women's activism as supportive rather than central to movement strategy. Baker's emphasis on female leadership threatened traditional gender roles and challenged assumptions about appropriate behavior for women activists.

But Baker's feminist organizing also proved remarkably effective at building sustainable movements and developing innovative strategies for social change. The women leaders she mentored often demonstrated exceptional skill at community organizing, coalition building, and long-term strategic planning that complemented and sometimes exceeded the contributions of their male counterparts.

Perhaps most importantly, Baker's feminist approach to organizing influenced an entire generation of women activists who carried her ideas into other social movements. Many of the women who later became leaders in feminist, environmental, and economic justice movements had learned their organizing skills from Baker or from women whom she had trained.

THE TEACHER OF TEACHERS

Figure 153: The legacy of Ella Baker lives on through the new generations of activists she inspired and trained.

As Ella Baker moved into her later career, she became increasingly focused on training new generations of organizers who could carry forward her philosophy of participatory democracy and grassroots organizing. She worked with universities, community organizations, and activist groups to develop educational programs that taught young people the skills and principles needed for effective social change work.

Baker's approach to organizer training emphasized practical skills like meeting facilitation, strategic planning, and coalition building. Still, it also focused on developing the political analysis and personal qualities that were necessary for sustained activism. She taught young organizers to listen carefully to community concerns, to build trust across different social groups, and to maintain hope and determination even when progress seemed impossible.

Most importantly, Baker taught organizers to see their role as developing other people's leadership rather than building their own prominence or power. She believed that the most effective organizers were those who made themselves unnecessary by helping communities develop the capacity to address their own problems.

Figure 154: Ella Baker empowers the next generation, turning strategy into shared strength.

This approach to organizer training influenced social justice movements far beyond civil rights. Environmental activists, immigrant rights organizers, labor union leaders, and community development workers adapted Baker's methods to their own campaigns and causes.

Baker's influence was particularly strong among women activists who were seeking alternatives to traditional leadership models that emphasized hierarchy, competition, and individual achievement. Her philosophy of collective leadership and participatory democracy provided a framework for feminist organizing that influenced the women's movement, environmental justice campaigns, and other social movements that emerged in the 1970s and 1980s.

By the time Baker died in 1986, her organizing philosophy had become so widely adopted that many activists used her methods without knowing their origin. The woman who had deliberately avoided publicity and celebrity had created a more influential legacy than many famous leaders whose names were widely recognized.

THE INVISIBLE REVOLUTION

Figure 155: Modern activists channel Ella Baker's legacy

Ella Baker's greatest achievement was not any single campaign or organization she helped build, but rather the transformation she brought to American ideas about democracy, leadership, and social change. Her philosophy of participatory democracy challenged fundamental assumptions about political power and provided alternative models for organizing that influenced multiple generations of activists.

Baker proved that ordinary people possessed the wisdom and capability to address complex social problems when they were given opportunities to work together and access to information about political processes. Her organizing successes demonstrated that sustainable social change came from developing the leadership capacity of entire communities rather than depending on exceptional individuals or established institutions.

Most importantly, Baker showed that democracy worked best when it included the voices and perspectives of people who had been traditionally excluded from decision-making processes. Her deliberate focus on developing female leadership, youth activism, and grassroots participation expanded American understanding of who could be effective political leaders.

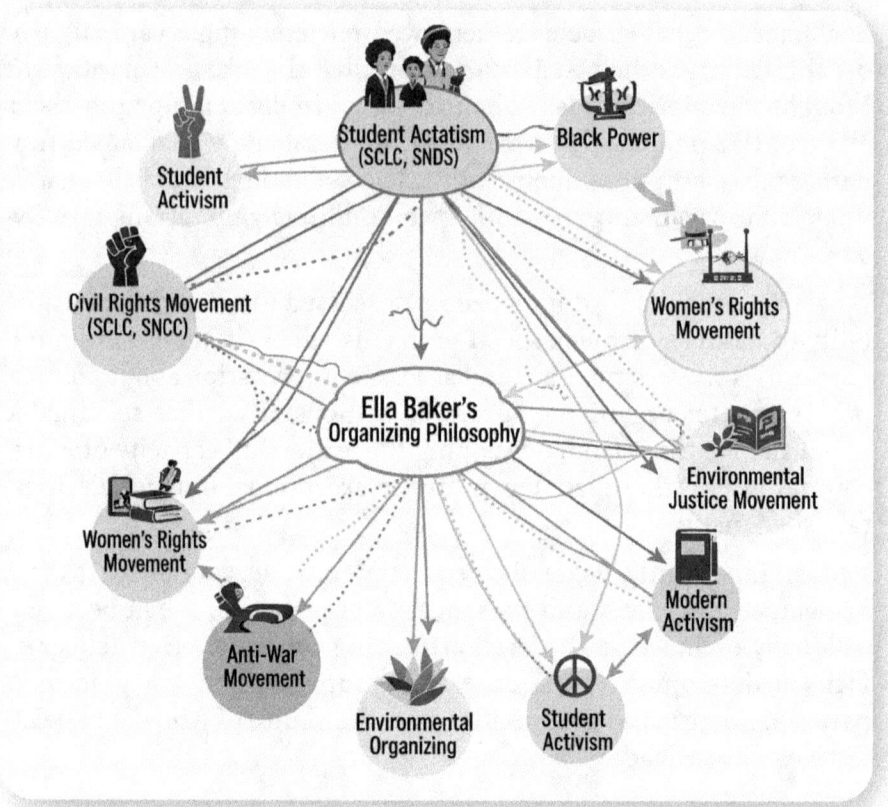

Figure 156: The influence of Ella Baker's organizing philosophy is a powerful thread that connects different social movements across generations.

The influence of Baker's organizing philosophy can be seen in contemporary social movements that emphasize collective leadership, participatory decision-making, and grassroots organizing. Environmental justice campaigns, immigrant rights movements, economic justice organizations, and even some electoral campaigns have adopted strategies that trace directly back to methods that Baker pioneered during her civil rights career.

But Baker's influence extends beyond specific organizing techniques to broader questions about democratic participation and social change. Her example demonstrates that effective leadership often involves making other people successful rather than building personal prominence, and that sustainable movements require developing institutional capacity rather than depending on charismatic personalities.

THE LEGACY OF EMPOWERMENT

Figure 157: Youth organizers today carry Ella Baker's torch

Today, Ella Baker is finally receiving recognition as one of the most important strategists and theorists in American civil rights history. Universities offer courses about her organizing philosophy, community organizations use her methods for leadership development, and activist networks study her approach to building sustainable movements.

But Baker's most important legacy isn't academic recognition or historical commemoration, it's the continuing influence of her organizing philosophy on social justice movements around the world. The young activists who are currently working on climate change, immigration reform, economic justice, and other pressing issues often use strategies and methods that Baker developed during her decades of civil rights organizing.

Her emphasis on developing grassroots leadership has proven particularly relevant to contemporary movements that must organize across diverse communities and address complex, interconnected social problems. Her focus on participatory democracy provides alternatives to traditional political approaches that many young activists find inadequate for addressing current challenges.

Figure 158: The vibrant spirit of democratic decision-making, as envisioned by Ella Baker, is alive and well in today's social movements.

Most importantly, Baker's example demonstrates that the people who change the world are often those who work quietly behind the scenes, building relationships, developing other people's leadership, and creating institutions that can sustain social change over time.

The woman who taught leaders how to lead understood that real power comes from empowering others, not from accumulating personal influence or recognition. Her legacy reminds us that the most important contributions to social progress are often made by people whose names never appear in history books but whose work creates the conditions that make visible achievements possible.

Ella Baker believed that the movement made Martin, not Martin the movement. Her life's work proved that the people who make movements possible are often the ones who never seek credit for their contributions, but who pour their talents into developing the collective capacity that allows entire communities to transform their own conditions.

In an era when American democracy faces unprecedented challenges, Ella Baker's vision of participatory democracy and grassroots organizing offers both inspiration and practical guidance for people who want to create meaningful social change. Her legacy reminds us that democracy works best when it includes everyone and that the most effective leaders often help others discover their leadership capacity.

Ella Baker's story reveals how real social change happens through patient organizing, relationship building, and collective leadership development rather than through charismatic personalities or dramatic public events. Her philosophy of participatory democracy challenged traditional assumptions about political power while providing practical methods for empowering marginalized communities to address their own problems. Baker's influence on civil rights organizing was profound but largely invisible, as she deliberately avoided publicity while training generations of activists who would carry her ideas into other social movements. Her legacy reminds us that the people who change the world are often those who work behind the scenes, developing other people's leadership and building institutions that can sustain social progress over time. In an era when democracy faces significant challenges, Baker's vision of grassroots organizing and collective leadership offers both inspiration and practical guidance for creating more inclusive and effective approaches to social change.

Part III:

The Crucible of Power: Presidential Leadership in Crisis

How presidents are really made

Chapter 9:
Lincoln's Rhetorical Genius

A HOUSE DIVIDED: WORDS AS WEAPONS AND HEALING

Figure 159: The eloquence of a great speaker is often the result of painstaking labor, as this image of Abraham Lincoln at his desk shows.

On November 19, 1863, as Abraham Lincoln rode the train from Washington to Gettysburg, Pennsylvania, he carried in his coat pocket a speech that would take him exactly two minutes to deliver. The organizers of the cemetery dedication had invited him almost as an afterthought; the main speaker would be Edward Everett, the most celebrated orator of his generation, who was expected to deliver a two-hour address befitting the occasion's solemnity.

Lincoln's role was ceremonial; his remarks were intended to be brief and forgettable. Instead, he was about to deliver 272 words that would become the most influential speech in American history.

But the Gettysburg Address wasn't a moment of sudden inspiration. It was the culmination of Lincoln's decades-long development as a strategic communicator who understood that in a democracy, the person who controls the narrative controls the nation. Lincoln had been using words as political weapons since his earliest days as a prairie lawyer. By 1863, he had become the most sophisticated rhetorical strategist ever to occupy the American presidency.

Figure 160: The somber landscape of Gettysburg, with its rows upon rows of graves, is a powerful reminder of the human cost of the Civil War, a cost that Lincoln sought to imbue with a profound national purpose.

Lincoln's genius wasn't just that he could write beautiful speeches, though his prose ranks among the finest in American literature. His genius was that he understood how language could reshape political reality, how the right words at the right moment could transform military defeats into moral victories, turn political opponents into fellow Americans, and convert a bloody civil war into a national rebirth.

At Gettysburg, Lincoln faced an impossible rhetorical challenge: how do you find meaning in a slaughter that had killed more than 50,000 Americans in three days? How do you honor the dead without glorifying war? How do you unite a divided nation while fighting a war that was literally tearing it apart?

His solution was to use language so carefully crafted, so strategically precise, that it would redefine not just the Civil War but the entire American experiment. In 272 words, Lincoln transformed a cemetery dedication into a national rededication, a battlefield commemoration into a constitutional convention, a moment of mourning into a call for rebirth.

The man who had once split rails was now splitting the difference between despair and hope, between division and unity, between the America that was and the America that could be.

THE PRAIRIE LAWYER'S LABORATORY

Figure 161: The humble frontier courtroom of Illinois was the training ground for the rhetorical skills that would one day shape a nation.

Abraham Lincoln's mastery of language didn't emerge from formal education or elite training; he had less than one year of formal schooling in his entire life. Instead, his rhetorical genius developed in the courtrooms and political meeting halls of frontier Illinois, where survival depended on your ability to persuade ordinary people to see complex issues your way.

As a young lawyer riding the judicial circuit through central Illinois, Lincoln learned that effective communication required understanding your audience better than they understood themselves. Frontier juries had little patience for flowery rhetoric or abstract legal arguments. They wanted speakers who could explain complicated ideas in plain language, find common ground between opposing viewpoints, and make them feel that their values and experiences were being respected.

Lincoln developed what would become his signature rhetorical style during these early years: simple vocabulary, concrete metaphors, logical progression of ideas, and an ability to find humor even in serious subjects. He learned to tell stories that made abstract principles concrete, to use biblical language that resonated with religious audiences without alienating secular listeners, and to frame political arguments in terms of shared American values rather than partisan positions.

Figure 162: The self-education of Abraham Lincoln, a testament to the power of a curious mind and the careful study of language.

But Lincoln's rhetorical education went far beyond courtroom experience. He was an obsessive student of language who read voraciously despite his limited formal education. He memorized passages from the Bible, Shakespeare, and John Bunyan's "Pilgrim's Progress," absorbing literary techniques that he would later adapt for political purposes.

Most importantly, Lincoln studied the speeches and writings of America's founding generation, particularly the Declaration of Independence and the Constitution. He understood that these documents had created a national political language that could be used to unite Americans around shared principles, even when they disagreed about specific policies.

This foundation in American political rhetoric would prove crucial during Lincoln's presidency, when he needed to speak simultaneously to multiple audiences, Union soldiers and Confederate sympathizers, radical abolitionists and conservative Republicans, foreign observers and future generations, while maintaining consistency and credibility with all of them.

The prairie lawyer who had learned to persuade Illinois farmers and frontier merchants was preparing himself, without knowing it, to persuade an entire nation to reimagine itself.

THE HOUSE DIVIDED STRATEGY

Figure 163: House Divided" speech was a powerful and controversial argument that shaped the course of American history.

Lincoln's emergence as a national political figure began with a speech that many advisors warned would destroy his career. On June 16, 1858, accepting the Republican nomination for U.S. Senate, Lincoln delivered an address that opened with one of the most famous lines in American political history: "A house divided against itself cannot stand."

The biblical quotation was familiar to his audience, but Lincoln's application of it to the slavery crisis was radical and risky. He argued that the United States could not continue to exist "half slave and half free," and that the nation would eventually become "all one thing, or all the other." This statement seemed to predict, and some critics argued, to advocate a violent resolution to the slavery question.

Lincoln's advisors begged him to remove the "house divided" language from his speech, arguing that it would alienate moderate voters who preferred compromise to confrontation. But Lincoln understood something about American political psychology that his cautious advisors missed: voters respond to leaders who name the crisis honestly in moments of genuine crisis rather than pretending it doesn't exist.

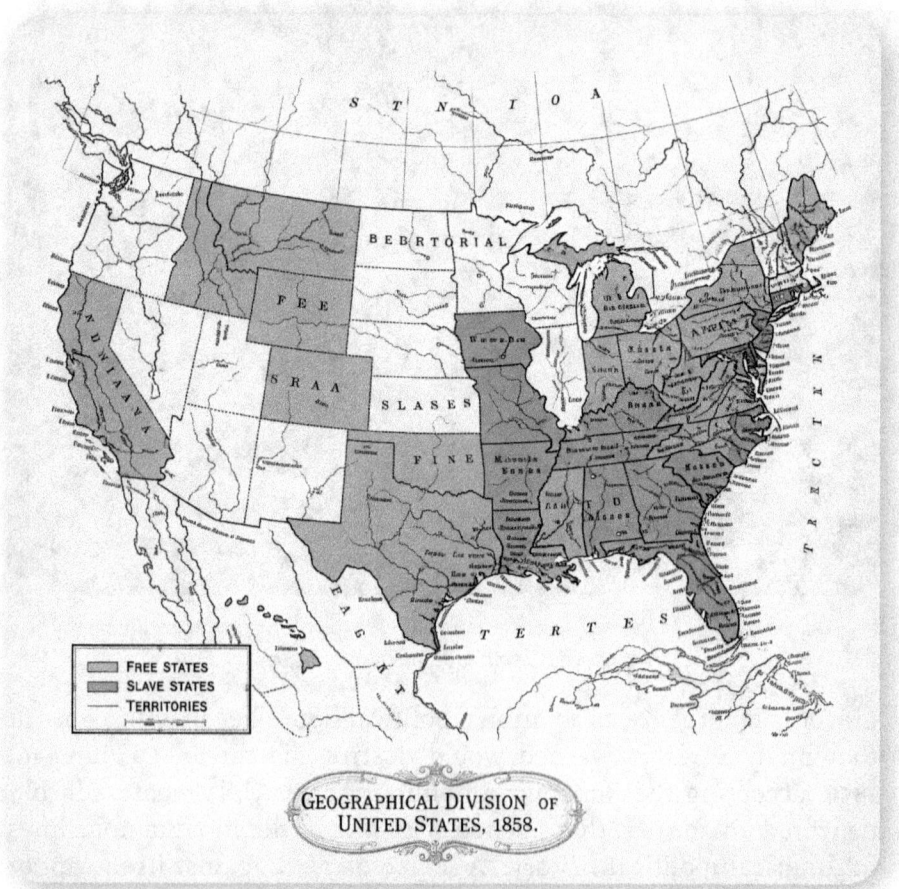

Figure 164: The map you requested shows the geographical division that Abraham Lincoln was addressing in his "House Divided" speech.

The rhetorical strategy behind the "House Divided" speech was sophisticated and deliberately provocative. Lincoln was forcing

Americans to confront the logical implications of their current political course, arguing that the Missouri Compromise and other attempts to balance slave and free interests were temporary measures that couldn't resolve the fundamental contradiction between American ideals of equality and the reality of human bondage.

By framing the slavery issue in biblical terms, Lincoln was appealing to religious voters who might otherwise avoid political controversy. By presenting the choice as inevitable rather than optional, he was positioning himself as someone who understood historical forces rather than someone who was trying to create unnecessary conflict.

Most importantly, Lincoln established himself as a leader who could articulate complex moral and political issues in language ordinary Americans could understand and accept. He was proving that he possessed the rhetorical skills needed to guide the nation through a crisis that would require extraordinary political communication.

The "House Divided" speech lost Lincoln the Senate election to Stephen Douglas, but it established him as a national Republican leader and positioned him for the presidential nomination in 1860. More importantly, it demonstrated his ability to use language strategically to reshape political debate and prepare public opinion for difficult choices that lay ahead.

THE FIRST INAUGURAL: WALKING THE TIGHTROPE

Figure 165: The presence of troops at Lincoln's first inauguration underscores the deep divisions that had already fractured the nation

When Abraham Lincoln delivered his first inaugural address on March 4, 1861, he faced a rhetorical challenge that no previous American president had confronted: how do you take the oath of office to preserve a union that is already dissolving? Seven states had seceded from the Union, Confederate forces were mobilizing, and many observers expected war to begin within days.

Lincoln's inaugural address had to accomplish multiple, potentially contradictory objectives simultaneously. He needed to reassure Unionists that he would defend federal authority while convincing secessionists that he posed no immediate threat to their interests. He had to demonstrate strength without appearing aggressive, show flexibility without seeming weak, and maintain hope for peaceful resolution while preparing the nation for possible war.

His rhetorical solution was to separate constitutional issues from personal animosity, arguing that political disagreements didn't require permanent separation. "We are not enemies, but friends," Lincoln declared. "We must not be enemies. Though passion may have strained, it must not break our bonds of affection."

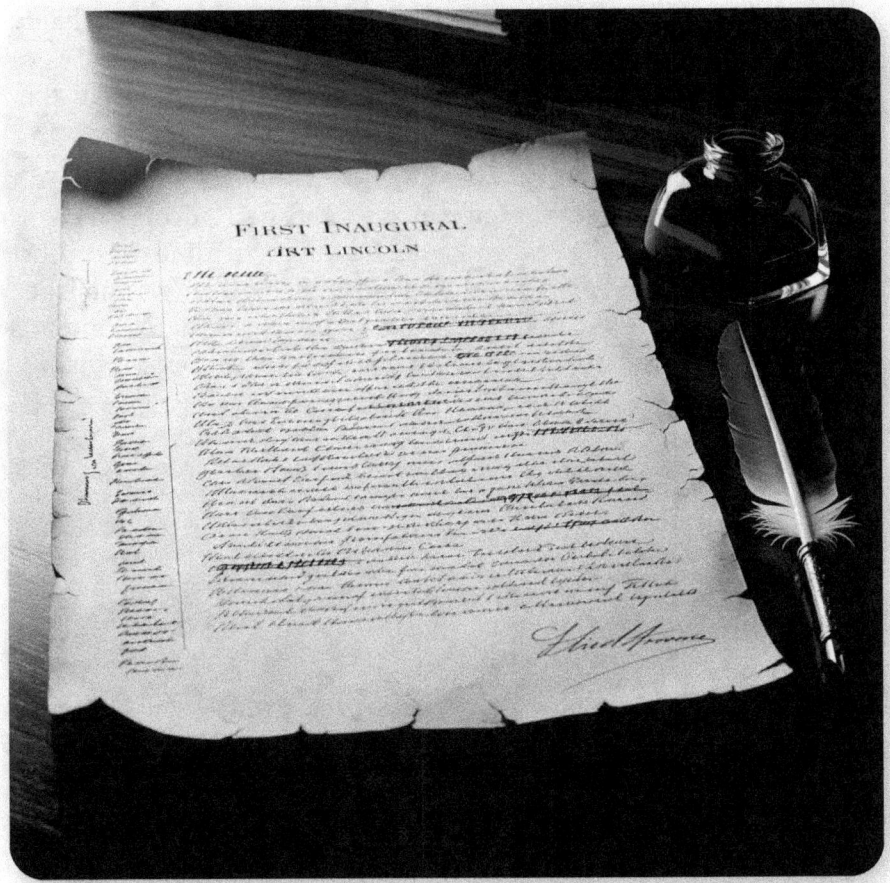

Figure 166: The painstaking revisions on the draft of Lincoln's First Inaugural Address show the immense care he took in crafting his words to unite a fractured nation.

The speech's most innovative rhetorical element was Lincoln's redefinition of the secession crisis as a misunderstanding rather than an irreconcilable conflict. He argued that Southerners had been misled about his intentions regarding slavery, and that honest communication could resolve their concerns without destroying the Union.

This framing allowed Lincoln to address Southern fears while maintaining his constitutional authority. He promised not to interfere with slavery where it already existed, but he also made clear that he would enforce federal law and protect federal property. He was offering a compromise on policy while refusing to compromise on principle.

Lincoln's first inaugural also demonstrated his growing mastery of what would become his signature rhetorical technique: using shared American values to bridge political divisions. He appealed to the Constitution, the Declaration of Independence, and the shared history that bound Americans together despite their current disagreements.

The speech didn't prevent war; Confederate forces attacked Fort Sumter just five weeks later. However, it established Lincoln's rhetorical authority and provided a framework for understanding the conflict that would follow. When war came, Lincoln had already established himself as someone who had tried every peaceful alternative and was fighting to preserve rather than destroy American democratic institutions.

THE EMANCIPATION PROCLAMATION: LAW AS LITERATURE

Figure 167 The Emancipation Proclamation was a monumental decision that forever changed the purpose of the Civil War.

On September 22, 1862, Abraham Lincoln announced that he would issue an Emancipation Proclamation freeing enslaved people in rebellious states, effective January 1, 1863. The decision represented the most dramatic expansion of presidential power in American history. Still, Lincoln's rhetorical challenge was to present this revolutionary act as a conservative measure necessary to preserve the Union.

The preliminary Emancipation Proclamation was written in deliberately dry, legalistic language that avoided the soaring rhetoric of

Lincoln's campaign speeches or his inaugural addresses. Critics then and since have noted that the document reads more like a military order than a charter of human freedom. But this apparent stylistic failure was actually a strategic rhetorical success.

By framing emancipation as a military necessity rather than a moral imperative, Lincoln was appealing to Northern voters who supported the war effort but remained skeptical about racial equality. He was transforming his presidency's most radical policy decision into a pragmatic response to the Confederate rebellion.

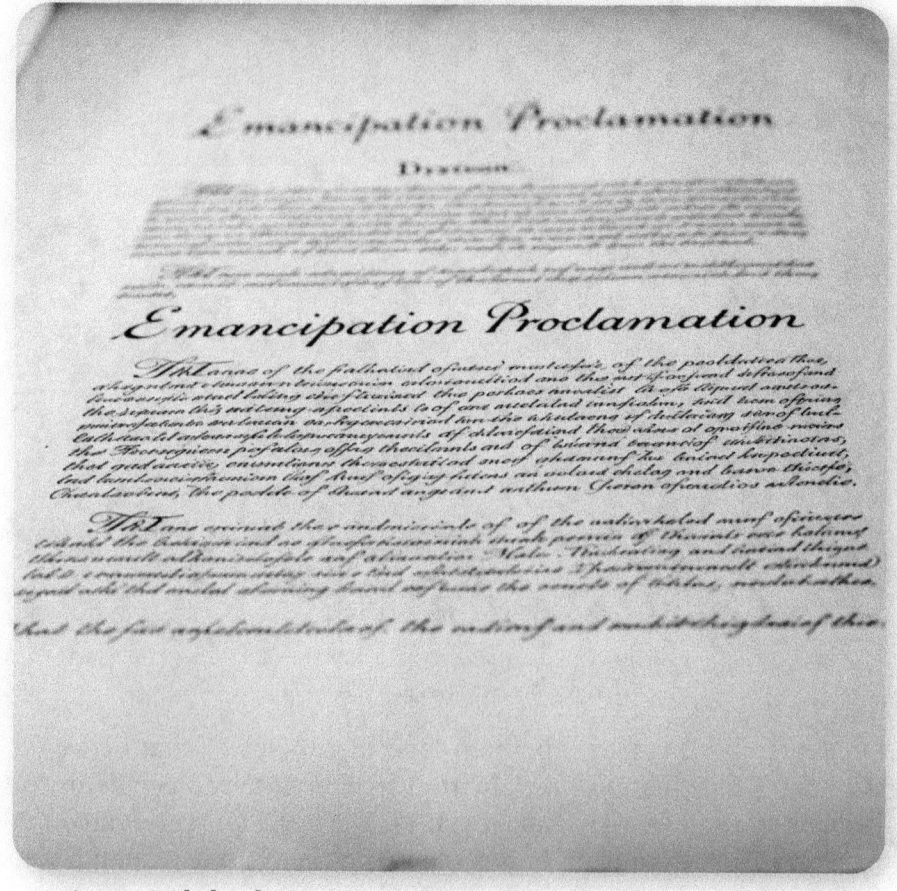

Figure 168: The handwritten Emancipation Proclamation document, showcasing Abraham Lincoln's careful legal language and strategic timing.

The rhetorical genius of the Emancipation Proclamation lay not in its inspiring language but in its careful limitation of scope. Lincoln freed enslaved people only in areas "in rebellion against the United States," leaving slavery untouched in border states that remained loyal to the Union. This geographical limitation made emancipation appear to be a punishment for Confederate resistance rather than a general assault on the institution of slavery.

More importantly, Lincoln grounded his emancipation authority in his role as commander-in-chief rather than appealing to abstract principles of human equality. This constitutional framing protected him from charges that he was exceeding presidential authority while allowing him to present emancipation as a necessary war measure.

The result was a document that simultaneously freed nearly four million people from bondage while maintaining the political coalition needed to win the war. Lincoln had used precise legal language to accomplish a moral revolution while preserving his ability to govern effectively.

But Lincoln understood that the Emancipation Proclamation's legalistic language was insufficient for the historical moment's moral significance. Ten months later, at Gettysburg, he would provide the soaring rhetoric that the liberation moment deserved, connecting emancipation to America's founding principles and future possibilities.

GETTYSBURG: THE ALCHEMY OF LANGUAGE

Figure 169: Lincoln rises quietly at Gettysburg, his slight frame bearing words that would echo through history.

The Gettysburg Address accomplished something that most observers considered impossible: it transformed America's bloodiest battle into a moment of national redemption. In 272 words delivered in less than three minutes, Lincoln redefined the Civil War's meaning, rededicated the nation to principles of equality, and created a new framework for understanding American democracy.

Lincoln's rhetorical strategy at Gettysburg was revolutionary in its simplicity. Instead of describing the battle or honoring specific heroes, he argued that the living could not consecrate a battlefield that had already been consecrated by those who died there. This rhetorical move allowed him to shift focus from past sacrifice to future responsibility.

"It is for us the living, rather, to be dedicated here to the unfinished work which they who fought here have thus far so nobly advanced." With this sentence, Lincoln transformed a memorial service into a re-dedication ceremony, a moment of mourning into a call for renewed commitment to the principles for which the battle had been fought.

Figure 170: The words of the Gettysburg Address, though few, carried a weight that transformed the meaning of the Civil War.

The address's most famous phrase, "government of the people, by the people, for the people", was more than inspiring rhetoric. It was a redefinition of American democracy that expanded beyond the Constitution's original framework. Lincoln was arguing that the Civil War had created a new birth of freedom that would fulfill the Declaration of Independence's promise of equality for all people.

Lincoln's most important rhetorical achievement was this connection between the Civil War and the American founding. He argued that the soldiers who died at Gettysburg were completing the work begun by the founders in 1776, fulfilling the promise of equality that the original Constitution had left incomplete.

By framing the war as a fulfillment of American founding principles rather than a departure from them, Lincoln provided moral justification for the enormous sacrifices that victory would require. He was also preparing the groundwork for Reconstruction policies that would extend full citizenship to formerly enslaved people.

The Gettysburg Address proved that Lincoln had become more than a skilled political communicator; he had become a master of what might be called democratic rhetoric, language that could unite diverse audiences around shared values while inspiring them to sacrifice for ideals larger than their immediate interests.

THE SECOND INAUGURAL: MALICE TOWARD NONE

Figure 171: With the war nearing its end, the massive crowd gathered for Lincoln's Second Inaugural Address reflected a nation on the brink of transformation.

Abraham Lincoln's Second Inaugural Address, delivered on March 4, 1865, with Union victory almost assured, presented him with a rhetorical challenge that was in some ways more difficult than those he had faced during the war's darkest moments. How do you prepare a victorious nation for the moral complexities of peace? How do you call for reconciliation without minimizing the moral stakes that had justified four years of unprecedented carnage?

Lincoln's solution was to frame the Civil War as a form of divine judgment that had punished both North and South for the sin of slavery. "If we shall suppose that American slavery is one of those offenses which, in the providence of God, must needs come, but which, having continued through His appointed time, He now wills to remove, and that He gives to both North and South this terrible war as the woe due to those by whom the offense came, shall we discern therein any departure from those divine attributes which the believers in a living God always ascribe to Him?"

This theological interpretation of the war allowed Lincoln to call for reconciliation without minimizing the moral dimensions of the conflict. Both North and South had been punished for their participation in slavery, and both could now work together to heal the wounds that the war had created.

Figure 172: The crowd at Lincoln's Second Inaugural, a mix of Union soldiers and civilians, reflected a nation gathering to hear his vision for peace and reconciliation.

The address's most famous passage, "With malice toward none, with charity for all, with firmness in the right as God gives us to see the right, let us strive on to finish the work we are in, to bind up the nation's wounds", was not just inspiring rhetoric but strategic political communication. Lincoln was preparing Northern audiences for Reconstruction policies that would emphasize restoration rather than punishment, while reassuring Southern audiences that reunion was possible despite their rebellion.

But Lincoln's call for reconciliation came with an important condition: "firmness in the right as God gives us to see the right." He was not advocating moral relativism or suggesting that the Union and Confederacy had been equally justified. Instead, he was arguing that true reconciliation required acknowledgment of moral reality, slavery was wrong, and its abolition was right, while also recognizing that healing would require generosity rather than vengeance.

The Second Inaugural demonstrated Lincoln's evolution as a rhetorical strategist who could address the most complex moral and political questions with language that was simultaneously principled and practical, inspiring and realistic, firm and generous.

THE UNDELIVERED SPEECH

Figure 173: The incomplete speech draft on Lincoln's desk represents the reconstruction vision that died with him, a testament to the tragic loss of his leadership.

On the evening of April 14, 1865, Abraham Lincoln was carrying the draft of a speech he planned to deliver about Reconstruction policies in his pocket. The address would have outlined his vision for reuniting the nation while extending full citizenship rights to formerly enslaved people. Instead, John Wilkes Booth's bullet ensured that Lincoln's final rhetorical masterpiece would never be delivered.

The fragments that survive of Lincoln's planned Reconstruction speech suggest that he was preparing to use his rhetorical skills to accomplish perhaps his most difficult political challenge: convincing war-weary Americans to support the difficult work of building a truly integrated democracy. He would have had to argue for policies that went far beyond what most Northern voters had supported when the war began, while maintaining the political coalition needed to implement those policies effectively.

Lincoln's assassination meant that Reconstruction would proceed without the rhetorical leadership that had guided the nation through the war. His successor, Andrew Johnson, lacked both Lincoln's political skills and his commitment to racial equality, leading to Reconstruction policies that failed to fulfill the promise of emancipation.

Figure 174: Ford's Theatre, on the night of April 14, 1865, where a nation's leader and his rhetorical genius were tragically silenced.

The loss of Lincoln's rhetorical leadership had consequences that extended far beyond his individual death. The man who had used language to redefine American democracy and prepare the nation for unprecedented change would not be available to guide the even more complex process of creating a truly integrated society.

But Lincoln's rhetorical legacy continued to influence American political discourse long after his death. His speeches provided a framework for understanding American democracy that future leaders could draw upon when facing their own crises. His example of using language to unite rather than divide, to inspire rather than manipulate, to call Americans to their better angels rather than appealing to their worst instincts, established standards for presidential communication that continue to influence political rhetoric today.

THE RHETORICAL PRESIDENCY

Figure 175: The legacy of Abraham Lincoln's rhetorical model continues to influence leaders today, as seen in this image.

Abraham Lincoln essentially invented what historians now call "the rhetorical presidency", the idea that presidents govern primarily through their ability to communicate with the American people rather than through administrative efficiency or legislative maneuvering. Before Lincoln, most presidents viewed public speaking as a relatively minor part of their responsibilities. After Lincoln, effective communication became essential to presidential success.

Lincoln proved that in a democracy, the person who controls the narrative often controls political reality. His ability to frame complex issues in language that ordinary Americans could understand and accept allowed him to build public support for policies that might otherwise have been impossible to implement.

Most importantly, Lincoln demonstrated that presidential rhetoric could be both inspiring and strategic, appealing to Americans' highest ideals while also accomplishing practical political objectives. His speeches didn't just move audiences emotionally; they prepared public opinion for difficult decisions and built political coalitions that could sustain policy changes over time.

Figure 176: The enduring legacy of Abraham Lincoln's speeches continues to shape American political rhetoric, inspiring new generations of leaders and citizens alike.

But Lincoln's rhetorical legacy also established expectations for presidential communication that proved difficult for his successors to meet. The man who had used language to guide the nation through its greatest crisis set a standard for presidential eloquence and moral leadership that few presidents have been able to match.

His example reminds us that effective democratic leadership requires more than policy expertise or political skill; it requires the ability to help citizens understand their choices and inspire them to sacrifice for ideals larger than their immediate interests. Lincoln's rhetorical genius lay not just in his ability to write beautiful speeches but in his understanding that in a democracy, the most important battles are often fought with words rather than weapons.

The prairie lawyer who had learned to persuade Illinois juries became the president who persuaded an entire nation to reimagine itself. His words didn't just describe American democracy; they created new possibilities for what American democracy could become.

WORDS THAT CHANGED THE WORLD

Figure 177: The timeless words of Abraham Lincoln, carved in stone, continue to inspire and guide Americans from all walks of life.

Abraham Lincoln's rhetorical achievement was unprecedented in American history and remains unmatched by any subsequent president. In speeches that totaled fewer than 10,000 words, he redefined American democracy, provided moral justification for the Civil War, prepared the nation for emancipation, and created a framework for understanding American ideals that continues to influence political discourse today.

Lincoln's rhetorical genius lay not just in his beautiful prose or inspiring ideas, but in his strategic understanding of how language could reshape political reality. He used words to build coalitions, prepare public opinion for difficult decisions, and unite diverse audiences around shared values.

Most importantly, Lincoln proved that effective presidential communication required more than political skill or oratorical ability; it required moral clarity, intellectual honesty, and genuine respect for the intelligence and judgment of ordinary citizens. His speeches succeeded because they treated Americans as capable of understanding complex issues and making difficult choices when those issues were explained clearly and honestly.

Figure 178: The enduring legacy of Abraham Lincoln's speeches continues to shape American political rhetoric, inspiring new generations of leaders and citizens alike.

Lincoln's rhetorical legacy reminds us that in a democracy, leadership is ultimately about persuasion rather than coercion, inspiration rather than manipulation, and appealing to citizens' better angels rather than their worst instincts. His example establishes standards for presidential communication that remain relevant today, when American democracy faces new challenges requiring the kind of moral clarity and rhetorical skill Lincoln brought to his own era's crises.

The man who used words to save the Union proved that in America, the pen can indeed be mightier than the sword when it's wielded with the skill, wisdom, and moral courage that democratic leadership requires.

Abraham Lincoln's rhetorical genius transformed the American presidency and established new possibilities for democratic leadership through effective communication. His speeches didn't just respond to the crises of his era; they helped create new frameworks for understanding American democracy and citizenship that continue to influence political discourse today. Lincoln proved that presidential rhetoric could be both inspiring and strategic, appealing to Americans' highest ideals while accomplishing practical political objectives. His example reminds us that effective democratic leadership requires the ability to help citizens understand their choices and inspire them to sacrifice for ideals larger than their immediate interests. In an era when American democracy faces new challenges, Lincoln's rhetorical legacy provides both inspiration and practical guidance for leaders who must use words to build coalitions, prepare public opinion for difficult decisions, and unite diverse audiences around shared values.

Chapter 10:
FDR's Triple Crisis

MANAGING DEPRESSION, DROUGHT, AND DICTATORS

Figure 179: In 1933, FDR faced the weight of a collapsing world—banks failing, drought spreading, and dictators rising

On the morning of March 4, 1933, as Franklin Delano Roosevelt prepared to take the presidential oath of office, America faced three simultaneous crises that threatened the survival of democratic capitalism. The Great Depression had closed every bank in the nation and left 25% of Americans unemployed. The worst drought in recorded history was turning the Great Plains into a dust bowl that was forcing millions of farmers to abandon their land. And in Germany, Adolf Hitler had just seized power and was beginning his transformation of Europe into a fascist empire.

Any one of these crises would have challenged the most experienced president. Together, they presented challenges that seemed to exceed the capacity of democratic government itself. Millions of Americans were beginning to wonder whether democracy and capitalism were failed experiments, whether the future belonged to the communist system emerging in Soviet Russia or the fascist regimes taking power in Germany and Italy.

Roosevelt understood that he wasn't just inheriting policy problems but a crisis of confidence in American democratic institutions. His inaugural address would have to restore faith in the government's ability to solve problems. In contrast, his administration would have to prove that democracy could be as effective as dictatorship in responding to national emergencies.

Figure 180: The human suffering and quiet desperation of the Great Depression

But Roosevelt brought to the presidency a unique combination of personal experience with adversity, political skills honed during two decades of public service, and an innovative understanding of how mass communication could be used to build public support for governmental action. The man who had learned to function despite being paralyzed by polio was about to teach America how to function despite being paralyzed by economic collapse, environmental disaster, and international crisis.

Roosevelt's response to the triple crisis would transform not just the American government but American society itself. His presidency would establish new expectations about federal responsibility for economic security, environmental protection, and international leadership that continue to influence American politics today.

Most importantly, Roosevelt would prove that democratic leadership could be both effective and humane, that governments could respond to crises without abandoning democratic principles or constitutional limitations. In an era when dictatorships seemed to offer efficiency and certainty, Roosevelt would demonstrate that democracy's flexibility and openness were actually advantages rather than weaknesses.

THE PARALYZED PRESIDENT

Figure 181: Roosevelt in quiet defiance, leading a nation while seated in strength

Franklin Roosevelt's polio diagnosis in 1921 had prepared him for the presidency in ways that no formal political training could have accomplished. At age 39, he had been a rising political star with a bright future when the disease paralyzed his legs and seemed to end his career permanently. His struggle to rebuild his life and return to politics had taught him lessons about crisis management, personal resilience, and the psychology of hope that would prove invaluable during his presidency.

Roosevelt's disability also gave him insights into suffering and vulnerability that few politicians of his privileged background possessed.

He understood what it meant to have your world collapse suddenly, face insurmountable challenges, and rebuild your life from a position of apparent weakness. These experiences had developed his capacity for empathy with ordinary Americans who were facing their own crises during the Depression.

But perhaps most importantly, Roosevelt's disability had taught him the importance of maintaining public confidence even in the face of private uncertainty. He had spent twelve years carefully managing his public image to hide the extent of his paralysis, understanding that political effectiveness required projecting strength and optimism even when facing enormous personal challenges.

Figure 182: Roosevelt rallies the nation in 1932, standing tall with hidden braces and unshakable resolve.

This experience with image management would prove crucial during his presidency, when Roosevelt needed to project confidence and competence while dealing with problems that had no obvious solutions. He had learned that leadership often required performing strength rather than simply possessing it, and that public confidence could be maintained through careful communication even during periods of genuine uncertainty.

Roosevelt's personal struggle with disability had also developed his skills as a strategic thinker who could adapt to changing circumstances rather than following rigid ideological prescriptions. He had learned to be pragmatic about methods while remaining consistent about goals, to experiment with different approaches rather than assuming that any single strategy would solve complex problems.

These qualities, empathy, strategic communication, adaptive thinking, and patient experimentation, would become the hallmarks of Roosevelt's presidential leadership and the foundation of his success in managing multiple simultaneous crises.

THE BANKING CRISIS: DEMOCRACY VS. EFFICIENCY

Figure 183: The crowds gathered outside closed banks in 1933 represented the immediate financial crisis

When Roosevelt took office on March 4, 1933, the American banking system had essentially ceased functioning. Panic withdrawals had forced governors in 38 states to declare "bank holidays" that closed financial institutions and left millions of Americans without access to their savings. The previous week had seen the collapse of major banks in New York and Chicago, and many observers expected the entire capitalist system to fail within days.

Roosevelt's advisors urged him to declare a national emergency and assume dictatorial powers that would allow him to reorganize the banking system without congressional approval. Similar crisis responses were being implemented by fascist governments in Europe, where democratic institutions were being suspended in favor of emergency rule by strongmen who promised efficiency and decisive action.

Instead, Roosevelt chose a response that demonstrated democracy's capacity for effective crisis management while maintaining constitutional processes and public accountability. He declared a four-day "bank holiday" that closed all financial institutions temporarily. Still, he also called Congress into special session and asked for legislation that would provide systematic solutions to the banking crisis.

Figure 184: FDR signs the Emergency Banking Act, surrounded by lawmakers—democracy at work in a time of crisis.

More importantly, Roosevelt used the crisis as an opportunity to demonstrate a new form of presidential communication that could build public confidence through honest explanation rather than false reassurance. On March 12, 1933, he delivered the first of his famous "Fireside Chats", radio addresses that spoke directly to ordinary Americans about complex policy issues in language they could understand.

The first Fireside Chat focused entirely on the banking crisis. Roosevelt explained in simple terms why banks had failed, what his administration was doing to fix the problems, and why Americans could safely return their money to banks when they reopened. He avoided both technical jargon and false optimism, instead treating his audience as intelligent citizens who could handle honest information about serious problems.

"I want to tell you what has been done in the last few days, why it was done, and what the next steps are going to be," Roosevelt began. He went on to explain the mechanics of banking in terms that any ordinary American could understand, building public confidence through education rather than manipulation.

The results were immediate and dramatic. When banks reopened on March 13, deposits exceeded withdrawals for the first time in months, as Americans responded to Roosevelt's honest communication by restoring their faith in the banking system. The president had proven that democratic leadership could be both transparent and effective, building public support through explanation rather than demanding blind trust.

THE DUST BOWL: ENVIRONMENTAL CATASTROPHE AS POLITICAL CHALLENGE

Figure 185: The immense dust storms of the Dust Bowl were an environmental disaster that displaced millions of Americans.

While Roosevelt was addressing the banking crisis, an environmental catastrophe was unfolding across the Great Plains that would test his administration's ability to respond to problems that seemed beyond governmental control. The Dust Bowl drought had begun in 1930. It was intensifying each year, turning millions of acres of farmland into desert and forcing hundreds of thousands of families to abandon their homes.

The drought was more than an environmental problem; it was an economic and social catastrophe destroying rural communities, overwhelming urban areas with desperate refugees, and challenging fundamental assumptions about American progress and prosperity. The images of dust storms that buried entire towns and displaced families loading their possessions onto trucks became symbols of American vulnerability that fascist propagandists used to argue that democracy was unable to provide basic security for its citizens.

Roosevelt's response to the Dust Bowl revealed his administration's innovative approach to problems that required long-term thinking rather than immediate solutions. Unlike the banking crisis, which could be addressed through legislation and regulation, the environmental disaster required new forms of governmental action that had no precedent in American history.

Figure 186: The Civilian Conservation Corps, a key part of Roosevelt's New Deal, put millions of young men to work on vital environmental restoration projects.

The administration's environmental programs combined immediate relief for displaced families with long-term strategies for preventing future ecological disasters. The Civilian Conservation Corps employed young men to plant trees and build soil conservation projects that would restore damaged ecosystems over decades. The Soil Conservation Service developed new farming techniques that could prevent erosion and maintain productivity even during drought periods.

But Roosevelt's most important response to the Dust Bowl was his recognition that environmental problems required federal coordination and resources that exceeded the capacity of state and local governments. He was essentially creating a new understanding of federal responsibility, including environmental protection and natural resource management as essential governmental functions.

This expansion of federal authority was controversial and faced significant political opposition from conservatives who argued that private initiative, rather than government programs, should address environmental problems. Roosevelt's response was to frame environmental protection as essential to national security and economic stability, arguing that governments had responsibilities to future generations that exceeded immediate political concerns.

The Dust Bowl programs established precedents for federal environmental action that would influence American policy for decades. Roosevelt proved that democratic governments could address long-term problems through patient, sustained effort rather than relying on crisis-driven responses or market-based solutions.

THE DICTATOR PROBLEM: DEMOCRACY UNDER SIEGE

Figure 187: 1930s headlines reveal a world in turmoil—fascism rising abroad as America fights to survive at home

As Roosevelt dealt with domestic crises, international developments were creating new challenges that would ultimately reshape American foreign policy and test democracy's ability to compete with totalitarian efficiency. Hitler's rise to power in Germany was followed by similar fascist movements in Italy, Spain, and Japan, creating a global trend toward authoritarian government that many observers considered historically inevitable.

The success of fascist governments in mobilizing their societies for economic recovery and military expansion posed a direct challenge to Roosevelt's democratic approach to crisis management. Hitler had eliminated unemployment in Germany through massive public works programs and military spending, while Mussolini had restored order and efficiency to the Italian government through dictatorial control.

These apparent successes led many Americans to question whether democracy was adequate for addressing modern challenges. Prominent businessmen, intellectuals, and politicians argued that America needed stronger executive authority and reduced congressional oversight if it hoped to compete with more efficient authoritarian systems.

Roosevelt's response to these challenges revealed his sophisticated understanding of how democratic leadership could be both effective and inspirational without abandoning constitutional principles. He refused to seek dictatorial powers even when facing unprecedented crises, instead working through existing institutions while expanding their capacity for coordinated action.

More importantly, Roosevelt used his communication skills to explain why democratic methods were actually superior to authoritarian alternatives, even when they appeared less efficient. He argued that democracy's openness to criticism and debate ultimately produced better policies than systems that depended on single leaders making decisions without input from diverse perspectives.

Roosevelt's Fireside Chats became a form of democratic theater, demonstrating how leaders could maintain public confidence through honest communication rather than propaganda and intimidation. While Hitler and Mussolini used mass rallies and choreographed spectacles to demonstrate their power, Roosevelt sat in his study and spoke conversationally to families gathered around their radios.

This intimate, personal approach to political communication proved remarkably effective at building trust and maintaining public support even during periods of genuine uncertainty about policy outcomes. Roosevelt was proving that democratic leadership could be both humble and strong, both accessible and authoritative.

THE NEW DEAL LABORATORY

Figure 188: The Workers Progress Administration was a New Deal program

Roosevelt's response to the triple crisis required creating new governmental institutions and policies that had no precedent in American history. The New Deal programs that emerged during his first term represented the most extensive expansion of federal authority since the Civil War, touching virtually every aspect of American economic and social life.

But Roosevelt's approach to policy innovation was deliberately experimental rather than ideological. He understood that unprecedented problems required untested solutions and was willing to try multiple approaches simultaneously rather than committing entirely to any single strategy.

This experimental method was reflected in the alphabet soup of New Deal agencies, the CCC, WPA, PWA, TVA, AAA, and dozens of others, each designed to address specific aspects of the multiple crises while contributing to overall recovery efforts. Some programs succeeded beyond expectations, others failed entirely, and many required constant modification as circumstances changed.

Figure 189: The vast scope and diversity of Roosevelt's experimental programs are illustrated in this map of New Deal projects across the United States.

Roosevelt's willingness to acknowledge failures and change course when programs weren't working demonstrated a form of leadership that was both humble and pragmatic. He famously told critics that if a program didn't work, he would try something else, treating policy-making as a form of scientific experimentation rather than ideological warfare.

This approach to governance required exceptional political skills, as Roosevelt had to maintain public and congressional support for expensive programs that might not produce immediate results. He used his communication abilities to explain why experimentation was necessary and why democratic governments needed flexibility to address complex problems.

Most importantly, Roosevelt's experimental approach to policy-making demonstrated that democratic governments could be innovative and adaptive rather than slow and bureaucratic. While authoritarian governments claimed efficiency through centralized decision-making, Roosevelt proved that democracy's openness to diverse ideas and willingness to change course could actually produce more effective solutions to complex problems.

THE RADIO PRESIDENT: INVENTING MODERN POLITICAL COMMUNICATION

Figure 190: A family gathered around their radio listening to a Fireside Chat

Franklin Roosevelt's mastery of radio communication represented a revolutionary development in presidential leadership that transformed how American leaders could build and maintain public support. The Fireside Chats, delivered irregularly throughout his presidency, created an unprecedented sense of personal connection between the president and citizens that allowed Roosevelt to maintain public confidence even during the most challenging periods of his administration.

Roosevelt's radio style was deliberately conversational and intimate, designed to make listeners feel that the president was speaking directly to them rather than delivering formal speeches to mass audiences. He used simple vocabulary, concrete examples, and personal anecdotes that made complex policy issues accessible to ordinary Americans regardless of their education or background.

But the Fireside Chats were more than effective communication; they were strategic political tools that allowed Roosevelt to build support for controversial policies by explaining them directly to voters rather than depending on newspaper coverage or congressional allies. He could bypass hostile media and opposition politicians by speaking directly to the American people about why his programs were necessary and how they would work.

Figure 191: Mastering the airwaves: FDR prepares to unite a nation through his Fireside Chat.

The political effectiveness of Roosevelt's radio communication was demonstrated repeatedly throughout his presidency. After each Fireside Chat, the White House would receive hundreds of thousands of letters from Americans expressing support for the president's policies and explaining how his programs had affected their personal situations.

This direct feedback from citizens provided Roosevelt with unprecedented insights into public opinion that allowed him to adjust his policies and communication strategies based on real-time information about how Americans were responding to his initiatives. He was essentially creating a new form of democratic dialogue that connected presidential leadership with grassroots opinion in ways that had never been possible before.

Roosevelt's radio mastery also demonstrated how new communication technologies could strengthen rather than undermine democratic institutions. While authoritarian leaders used radio and film for propaganda and indoctrination, Roosevelt used radio to educate citizens and build informed support for democratic policies.

The success of the Fireside Chats established expectations for presidential communication that continue to influence American politics today. Roosevelt had proven that effective democratic leadership required the ability to explain complex issues in accessible language and to maintain public confidence through honest, personal communication.

THE CRUCIBLE OF POWER: PRESIDENTIAL LEADERSHIP IN CRISIS

MANAGING MULTIPLE CRISES: THE ART OF PRESIDENTIAL ATTENTION

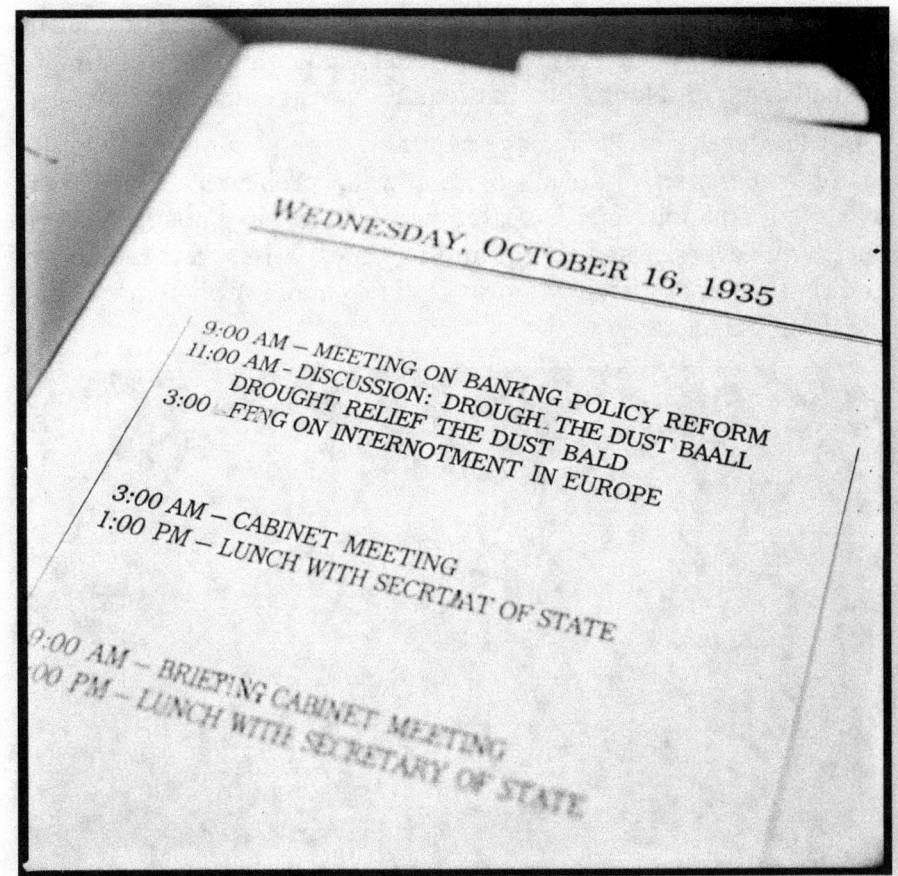

Figure 192: Roosevelt's schedule or calendar from 1935,

One of Roosevelt's most remarkable achievements was his ability to manage multiple serious crises simultaneously without losing focus on any single issue or allowing urgent problems to crowd out important long-term concerns. His daily schedule during the 1930s reveals a president who was constantly shifting attention between immediate emergencies and strategic planning, between domestic problems and international developments, between policy details and political communication.

Roosevelt's approach to crisis management required exceptional organizational skills and strategic thinking that allowed him to prioritize competing demands while maintaining progress on multiple fronts. He used his cabinet and White House staff as a coordinating mechanism that could handle routine decisions while keeping him informed about developments that required presidential attention.

But Roosevelt's crisis management also depended on his ability to maintain perspective during periods when problems seemed overwhelming and solutions appeared inadequate. His personal experience with adversity had taught him that most crises were temporary and that patient, sustained effort could overcome apparently insurmountable challenges.

Figure 193: A cabinet meeting during the 1930s showing Roosevelt coordinating responses to multiple simultaneous crises.

Perhaps most importantly, Roosevelt understood that managing multiple crises required maintaining public confidence and political support even when immediate solutions weren't available. He used his communication skills to help Americans understand that their government was actively working on their problems, even when results weren't immediately visible.

This approach to crisis communication was particularly important during the Dust Bowl drought, which continued for several years despite government intervention. Roosevelt had to maintain support for long-term environmental programs while acknowledging that immediate relief was limited and that recovery would require patience and sustained effort.

Roosevelt's success in managing the triple crisis proved that democratic leadership could be both comprehensive and effective, addressing multiple challenges simultaneously without sacrificing quality or abandoning constitutional processes. He had demonstrated that democracy's supposed inefficiency was actually a strength that allowed for coordinated responses to complex problems.

THE WAR THAT ENDED THE DEPRESSION

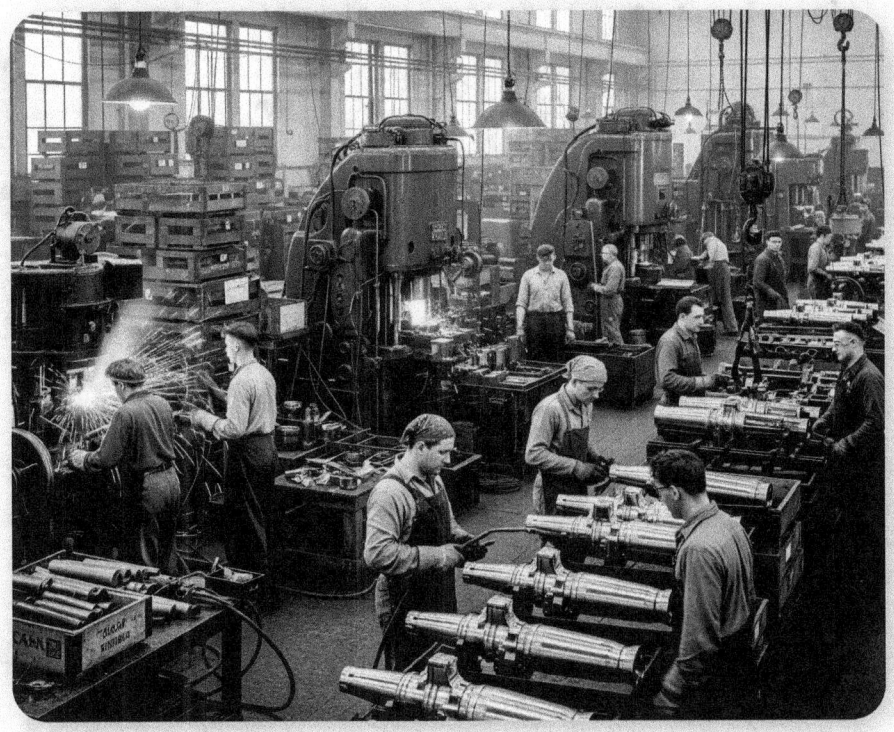

Figure 194: American factories converting to wartime production

The outbreak of World War II in Europe in September 1939 created new challenges for Roosevelt while also providing solutions to some of the domestic problems that had persisted throughout the 1930s. American military production for European allies began to reduce unemployment and stimulate economic growth in ways that New Deal programs had not been able to accomplish.

But the war also forced Roosevelt to balance competing priorities between domestic recovery and international responsibilities, between isolationist sentiment among American voters and the strategic necessity of supporting democratic allies against fascist aggression.

Roosevelt's response to these challenges revealed his evolution from a domestic policy president to a global leader who understood that American security and prosperity depended on international stability and democratic success abroad. He began preparing American public opinion for eventual participation in the war while maintaining the fiction that America could remain neutral in the global conflict.

Figure 195: Forging the Allied path: Roosevelt and Churchill in a pivotal moment of wartime diplomacy.

The transition from New Deal domestic programs to wartime mobilization demonstrated Roosevelt's flexibility as a leader who could adapt his priorities and strategies to changing circumstances without abandoning his fundamental commitment to democratic governance and social justice.

Roosevelt's management of America's entry into World War II proved that his crisis management skills were applicable to international and domestic challenges. The president who had learned to coordinate responses to economic depression, environmental disaster, and political upheaval could also coordinate the massive mobilization required for global warfare.

Most importantly, Roosevelt's wartime leadership validated his earlier arguments about democracy's advantages over authoritarian systems. American industrial capacity, technological innovation, and military effectiveness proved superior to fascist alternatives, demonstrating that democratic societies could be both humane and powerful when facing existential threats.

THE DEMOCRATIC ALTERNATIVE

Figure 196: FDR at Yalta in 1945, representing his role in creating the post-war international order based on democratic principles.

Franklin Roosevelt's presidency proved that democratic governments could respond effectively to existential crises without abandoning constitutional principles or democratic processes. His success in managing the triple crisis of depression, drought, and dictatorship demonstrated that democracy's flexibility and openness were actually advantages rather than weaknesses when facing complex challenges.

Roosevelt's experimental approach to policy-making, his innovative use of mass communication, and his ability to maintain public confidence during uncertain times established new models for democratic leadership that influenced American politics for generations. He had proven that democratic leaders could be both strong and humble, both decisive and accountable, both innovative and respectful of constitutional limitations.

Perhaps most importantly, Roosevelt's presidency demonstrated that effective crisis management required the skills and perspectives that only democratic societies could develop, the ability to synthesize diverse viewpoints, to admit mistakes and change course, to maintain public support through honest communication, and to balance competing interests while working toward common goals.

Figure 197: The continuing influence of Roosevelt's models of federal coordination in crisis management is evident in modern disaster response efforts.

Roosevelt's legacy reminds us that democratic leadership is not just about winning elections or implementing policies; it's about proving that democratic institutions can protect and serve their citizens during their greatest moments of need. His presidency established expectations about governmental responsibility and presidential leadership that continue to shape American politics today.

The man who had overcome personal paralysis to lead the nation through its greatest challenges since the Civil War proved that democracy's apparent weaknesses, its openness to criticism, its requirement for consensus-building, and its respect for individual rights were actually sources of strength that allowed democratic societies to adapt and thrive in the face of unprecedented challenges.

Franklin Roosevelt's management of the triple crisis validated democracy itself, proving that free societies could be as effective as dictatorships in responding to existential threats while maintaining the values and institutions that made life worth defending.

Franklin Roosevelt's presidency during the 1930s and early 1940s demonstrated that democratic leadership could effectively manage multiple existential crises simultaneously without abandoning constitutional principles or democratic processes. His innovative approaches to crisis communication, policy experimentation, and federal coordination established new models for presidential leadership that continue to influence American governance today. Roosevelt proved that democracy's supposed inefficiencies, openness to criticism, requirement for consensus-building, and respect for individual rights were strengths that allowed democratic societies to adapt and thrive when facing unprecedented challenges. His success in managing economic depression, environmental disaster, and the rise of global fascism validated democracy itself, showing that free societies could be both humane and effective when confronting threats to their survival. Roosevelt's legacy reminds us that effective democratic leadership requires not just political skill but also the ability to maintain public confidence through honest communication, to experiment with new solutions when traditional approaches prove inadequate, and to prove through action that democratic institutions can protect and serve their citizens during their greatest moments of need.

Chapter 11:
The President Nobody Expected to Lead

HOW GEORGE W. BUSH BECAME AMERICA'S VOICE ON 9/11

Figure 198: A quiet classroom, a children's book, and a president unaware—moments before the world would shift forever."

At 8:46 a.m. on September 11, 2001, George W. Bush was sitting in a second-grade classroom in Sarasota, Florida, listening to children read "The Pet Goat" when his chief of staff whispered in his ear: "A second plane hit the second tower. America is under attack."

For seven agonizing minutes, Bush remained seated with the children, his face a mask of controlled tension as he processed the implications of what he had just learned. Critics would later attack those seven minutes as evidence of indecision and weakness. But in that classroom, Bush was making calculations that would determine not just his presidency but America's response to the deadliest attack on American soil since Pearl Harbor.

Eight months into a presidency that many Americans viewed as illegitimate, he had lost the popular vote and won the Electoral College only after a controversial Supreme Court decision. Bush was widely considered an inexperienced leader who had been elevated beyond his capabilities. Critics portrayed him as an intellectual lightweight who depended on advisors to make important decisions. Foreign leaders questioned whether he possessed the gravitas and competence needed to lead the world's most powerful nation.

Figure 199: The view of the burning Twin Towers from Air Force One showed the magnitude of the crisis that would define a presidency.

September 11 changed everything. The attacks didn't just kill nearly 3,000 Americans and destroy iconic landmarks; they shattered the post-Cold War illusion that America was invulnerable to foreign threats and fundamentally safe from the conflicts that plagued other regions of the world.

In the hours and days following the attacks, Bush would be required to serve simultaneously as commander-in-chief, ordering military responses, consoler-in-chief, providing emotional leadership to a traumatized nation, and communicator-in-chief, explaining what had happened and what America would do in response.

The president who had been dismissed as unready for the challenges of leadership would discover within himself capabilities that surprised even his closest advisors. The man who had been criticized for lacking gravitas would find words that gave meaning to unprecedented tragedy. The leader who had been questioned for his intellectual depth would make decisions that would reshape American foreign policy for decades.

September 11 revealed that presidential leadership in crisis isn't just about preparation, experience, or intellectual brilliance; it's about finding within yourself the capacity to rise to occasions that no amount of training can fully prepare you.

THE UNLIKELY PRESIDENT

Figure 200: "President-Elect George W. Bush celebrates his hard-won 2000 victory—cheers echo, but so do questions."

George W. Bush entered the presidency under circumstances that would have challenged even the most experienced politician. The 2000 election had been the closest and most controversial in American history, decided by 537 votes in Florida after a recount battle that ended only when the Supreme Court effectively declared him the winner.

The bitter election fight had left the country deeply divided, with many Americans viewing Bush as an illegitimate president who had stolen the election through legal maneuvering rather than winning it through democratic processes. Democrats in Congress were prepared to treat him as a weak, temporary occupant of the White House rather than a legitimate leader with a mandate for major policy changes.

Bush's background seemed to confirm critics' arguments that he was unprepared for the presidency. His resume included business ventures of mixed success, a single term as governor of Texas, and no significant experience with foreign policy or national security issues. His public speaking often seemed uncertain, and his grasp of complex issues appeared superficial compared to predecessors like Bill Clinton, who had demonstrated mastery of policy details.

Figure 201: In early 2001, President George W. Bush meets with global leaders amid quiet skepticism over his diplomatic experience."

Even Bush's supporters had modest expectations for his presidency. They hoped he would be a competent manager who could work with Congress on domestic issues while relying on experienced advisors to handle foreign policy challenges. Few expected him to become a transformational leader who would reshape American foreign policy or demonstrate exceptional crisis leadership.

Bush's early months in office seemed to confirm these limited expectations. His first major international crisis, the collision between an American spy plane and a Chinese fighter jet in April 2001, was resolved through careful diplomacy that avoided escalation but didn't demonstrate exceptional presidential leadership. His domestic agenda focused on tax cuts and education reform, important but hardly revolutionary policy changes.

By summer 2001, Bush's approval ratings were modest, and his presidency seemed destined to be remembered as a caretaker administration that would serve one term before voters chose a more dynamic leader. Even his advisors privately worried that he lacked the political skills and intellectual curiosity needed to achieve significant accomplishments.

September 11 would prove how wrong those assessments were.

THE MOMENT OF TRUTH

Figure 202: President George W. Bush sits in a classroom at Emma E. Booker Elementary School in Sarasota, Florida

When Andrew Card whispered "America is under attack" in Bush's ear that Tuesday morning, the president faced an immediate test of leadership that no previous American president had confronted. The attacks were still unfolding, nobody knew how many more planes might be hijacked or what other targets might be struck, and Bush's responses in the next few hours would shape both the immediate crisis and America's long-term response to terrorism.

Bush's decision to remain in the classroom for several more minutes was later criticized as evidence of paralysis or confusion. Still, it actually demonstrated the kind of thoughtful restraint that effective crisis leadership requires. He understood that jumping up and rushing from the room would create panic among the children and signal to watching cameras that the president was out of control.

Instead, Bush used those seven minutes to think through his immediate priorities and begin developing a response strategy. He needed to project calm and competence while ensuring his own safety and establishing communication with his national security team. He had to balance the need for immediate action with the importance of gathering accurate information before making crucial decisions.

Figure 203: President Bush aboard Air Force One on 9/11, coordinating response amid crisis and urgency.

When Bush finally left the classroom, his actions demonstrated crisis leadership that surprised both critics and supporters. He quickly established communication with Vice President Cheney and other key advisors, authorized military aircraft to intercept any additional hijacked planes, and began coordinating the federal response to the attacks.

More importantly, Bush immediately understood that his role as president required him to provide emotional and symbolic leadership that went beyond operational crisis management. Within hours of the attacks, he was already thinking about how to address the nation and what messages would help Americans process the trauma they had experienced.

Bush's performance during the first day of the crisis revealed leadership capabilities that few observers had recognized. Under extreme pressure, he made clear, decisive choices while maintaining the composure and thoughtfulness that effective crisis management requires. The president who had been dismissed as inexperienced was demonstrating that real leadership often emerges only when it's desperately needed.

FINDING HIS VOICE

Figure 204: Bush addresses the nation on 9/11, marking his shift from uncertain politician to crisis leader.

Bush's address to the nation on the evening of September 11 marked a turning point both in his presidency and in his development as a leader. The speech he delivered that night was different in tone and substance from anything he had said during his political career, revealing communication skills and emotional depth that had been largely hidden during his first months in office.

"Today, our fellow citizens, our way of life, our very freedom came under attack in a series of deliberate and deadly terrorist acts," Bush began, his voice steady and his manner grave. The president, who had often seemed uncertain in formal speeches, was speaking with a clarity and authority that commanded attention and respect.

But the speech's most important element wasn't its formal rhetoric; it was Bush's ability to acknowledge the nation's pain while projecting confidence about America's response. He understood that Americans needed both validation of their shock and fear, and reassurance that their government could protect them and respond effectively to the attacks.

Figure 205: Americans gathered around their televisions on the evening of September 11

Bush's communication strategy after September 11 revealed his intuitive understanding of how presidents can provide emotional leadership during national crises. Unlike his predecessors, who had relied primarily on formal speeches and press conferences, Bush used a variety of communication formats that allowed him to connect with different audiences and address different aspects of the crisis.

His impromptu remarks at Ground Zero on September 14, delivered through a bullhorn while standing on the rubble of the World Trade Center, demonstrated his ability to provide symbolic leadership that transcended formal political communication. When someone in the crowd shouted that they couldn't hear him, Bush responded, "I can hear you. The rest of the world hears you. And the people who knocked these buildings down will hear all of us soon."

That moment captured something essential about effective crisis leadership: the ability to find exactly the right words at exactly the right time to express what an entire nation is feeling. Bush had discovered within himself a capacity for authentic emotional communication that nobody, including himself, had recognized before September 11.

THE DOCTRINE THAT CHANGED EVERYTHING

Figure 206: Bush addresses Congress on September 20, 2001, with bipartisan leaders standing behind him, symbolizing rare national unity in a time of crisis.

Bush's address to a joint session of Congress on September 20, 2001, established what would become known as the Bush Doctrine, a framework for American foreign policy that would reshape international relations for decades. The speech demonstrated strategic thinking and moral clarity that surprised observers who had questioned his intellectual capabilities.

"Either you are with us, or you are with the terrorists," Bush declared, articulating a worldview that would guide American foreign policy through two wars and multiple international interventions. This binary framework simplified complex international relationships and provided clear guidance for allies and enemies about American expectations and intentions.

The Bush Doctrine represented a fundamental departure from previous American foreign policy approaches that had emphasized multilateral cooperation and gradual diplomatic pressure. Instead, Bush was announcing that America would act unilaterally when necessary to protect its security interests and would hold other nations accountable for their responses to terrorism.

Figure 207: American troops begin military operations in Afghanistan, marking the swift execution of President Bush's new foreign policy.

Critics would later argue that the Bush Doctrine was overly simplistic and counterproductive, leading to military interventions that created more problems than they solved. But in the immediate aftermath of September 11, Bush's clear articulation of American intentions provided both domestic audiences and international observers with a framework for understanding how America would respond to the attacks.

Perhaps more importantly, the development of the Bush Doctrine revealed the president's evolution from a politician who had campaigned against "nation-building" and international interventions into a leader who understood that American security required active engagement with global threats.

This transformation wasn't just about policy changes; it reflected Bush's personal growth as a leader who had discovered that the presidency could call forth capabilities and convictions that had been dormant during his earlier political career. The attacks had forced him to think more deeply about America's role in the world and his own responsibilities as president.

THE CRUCIBLE OF POWER: PRESIDENTIAL LEADERSHIP IN CRISIS

THE RALLY EFFECT: LEADERSHIP THROUGH CRISIS

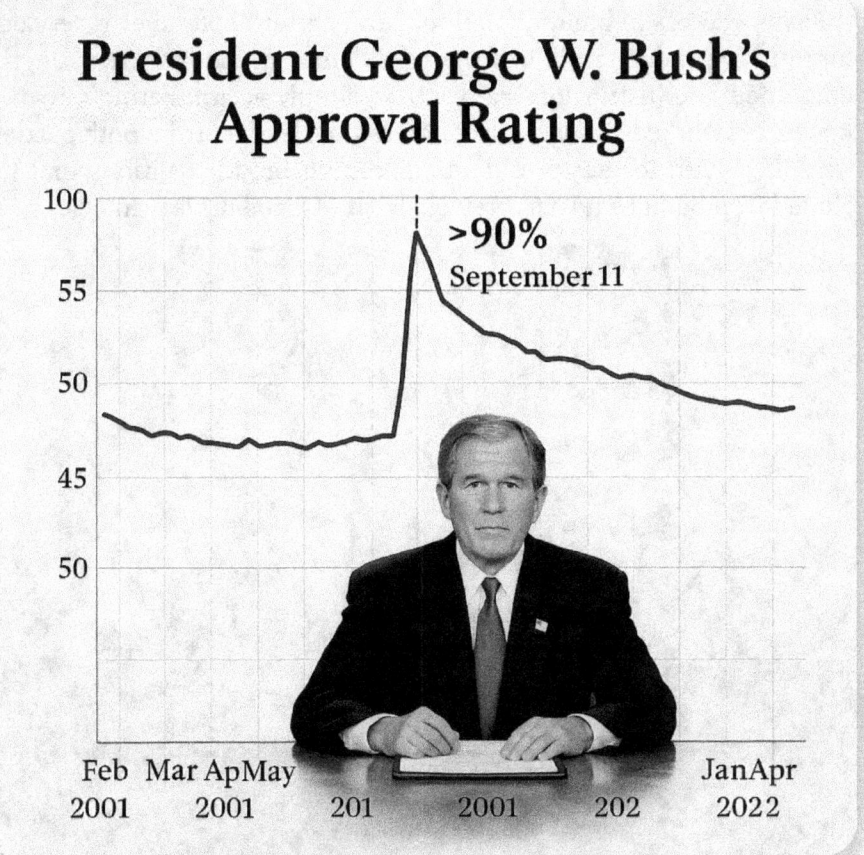

Figure 208: Bush's approval rating soared past 90% after 9/11, reflecting a rare moment of overwhelming national unity.

Bush's response to September 11 produced what political scientists call a "rally around the flag" effect that unified the country behind presidential leadership to a degree not seen since World War II. His approval ratings soared from the mid-50s to over 90%, making him one of the most popular presidents in American history.

But Bush's post-9/11 popularity wasn't just about Americans supporting their president during a crisis; it reflected genuine appreciation for leadership qualities that he had demonstrated under extreme pressure. The president, who had been criticized as inexperienced and unprepared, had provided exactly the kind of steady, determined leadership that the crisis required.

Bush's success in building national unity after September 11 revealed his intuitive understanding of how presidents can use crises to strengthen democratic institutions rather than simply accumulating personal power. He worked closely with congressional leaders from both parties, consulted with former presidents, and built broad coalitions that included Democrats who had previously questioned his legitimacy.

Figure 209: Bush meets with Democratic leaders Daschle and Gephardt, symbolizing post-9/11 bipartisan unity

More importantly, Bush used his enhanced political capital to pursue policies that he genuinely believed would protect American security rather than simply advancing partisan political goals. His proposals for new homeland security measures, military interventions, and intelligence reforms were based on strategic assessments rather than political calculations.

This approach to crisis leadership demonstrated Bush's personal integrity and his commitment to presidential responsibilities that transcended partisan politics. The president, whom the narrowest margin in American history had elected, was governing as if he had received a mandate from all Americans to protect their security and defend their values.

Bush's ability to maintain national unity and congressional support for more than two years after September 11 proved that effective crisis leadership can strengthen democratic institutions when presidents use their authority responsibly and maintain focus on national rather than partisan interests.

THE WEIGHT OF WAR

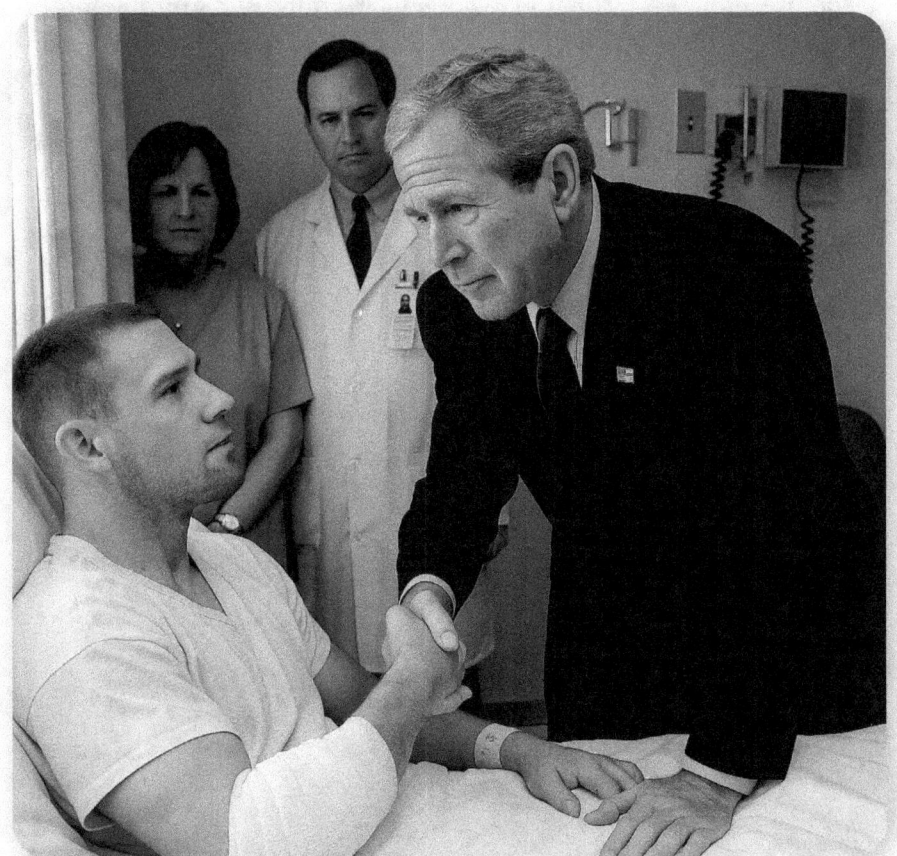

Figure 210: Bush visiting wounded soldiers at Walter Reed, reflecting the personal cost of war and the burden of presidential decisions.

The terrorist attacks thrust Bush into the role of wartime president. This responsibility would define the remainder of his presidency and test his leadership in ways that no peacetime challenges could have prepared him for. Within weeks of September 11, American forces were attacking Taliban strongholds in Afghanistan, beginning what would become the longest war in American history.

Bush's decision-making as commander-in-chief revealed both strengths and limitations that had been hidden during his first months in office. He demonstrated the kind of decisiveness and moral clarity that effective wartime leadership requires. Still, he also showed a tendency toward certainty that sometimes prevented him from adapting strategies when circumstances changed.

The president's personal involvement in military planning and his regular meetings with families of fallen soldiers demonstrated his understanding that wartime leadership carried moral responsibilities that extended far beyond policy decisions. He took personal responsibility for the consequences of his choices in ways that revealed the emotional burden of presidential authority.

Figure 211: Bush reviews strategic military plans with top generals, underscoring his active role in shaping wartime decisions.

But Bush's evolution as wartime president also revealed the dangers of presidential leadership that becomes too certain of its own correctness. His conviction that removing Saddam Hussein from power in Iraq was necessary for American security led to a war that proved far more difficult and costly than he had anticipated.

The Iraq War would ultimately damage Bush's historical reputation and demonstrate the limitations of the leadership style that had served him so well immediately after September 11. The qualities that made him effective during the initial crisis, decisiveness, moral clarity, and unwavering determination, became liabilities when applied to more complex problems that required flexibility and adaptation.

Bush's experience as wartime president illustrated both the possibilities and the dangers of crisis leadership. The same personal qualities that enabled him to provide exceptional leadership during a national emergency could also lead to costly mistakes when applied inappropriately to different kinds of challenges.

THE TRANSFORMATION THAT SURPRISED EVERYONE

Figure 212: Side-by-side images of George W. Bush before and after 9/11

The most remarkable aspect of Bush's post-9/11 leadership was how it completely transformed his presidency and his personal development as a political leader. The man who had seemed uncertain and inexperienced during his first months in office had discovered within himself capabilities that surprised even his closest advisors.

Bush's transformation wasn't just about learning new skills or gaining experience; it reflected a fundamental change in his understanding of presidential responsibility and his own leadership capacity. The attacks had forced him to confront challenges that revealed aspects of his character and abilities that had been dormant during his earlier political career.

This personal transformation was visible to everyone who worked with Bush before and after September 11. Advisors noted that he became more decisive, focused, and confident in his judgment. His public speaking improved dramatically as he found his authentic voice as a crisis leader. His strategic thinking became more sophisticated as he grappled with complex national security challenges.

Figure 213: Bush with his national security team in the White House Situation Room

Perhaps most importantly, Bush developed a sense of historical purpose that had been absent during his early presidency. He began to see his role not just as managing day-to-day governance but as protecting American security and values during a period of unprecedented threat.

This sense of mission gave Bush's presidency a focus and intensity that transformed his political effectiveness. The president, who had struggled to articulate his agenda during his first months in office, was now speaking with conviction about America's role in fighting global terrorism and protecting democratic values.

Bush's transformation after September 11 demonstrated that presidential leadership often emerges only when circumstances demand it. The attacks had called forth capabilities that might have remained hidden if his presidency had proceeded under normal circumstances.

THE PRICE OF CERTAINTY

Figure 214: Bush at his final press conference, visibly worn by the toll of eight years marked by war, crisis, and unrelenting leadership.

As Bush's presidency continued, the leadership qualities that had served him so well immediately after September 11 began to create new problems that would ultimately damage his historical reputation. His decisiveness became stubbornness, his moral clarity became inflexibility, and his confidence became overconfidence, preventing him from adapting to changing circumstances.

The Iraq War, in particular, revealed the limitations of Bush's crisis leadership style when applied to problems that required patience, flexibility, and willingness to change course based on new information. His conviction that removing Saddam Hussein was necessary for

American security led him to dismiss intelligence that contradicted his assumptions and to persist with strategies that weren't working.

Bush's experience demonstrated that the personal qualities that make leaders effective during one type of crisis may not be appropriate for different kinds of challenges. The decisiveness and certainty that Americans valued after September 11 became liabilities when dealing with the complex political and military challenges of nation-building in Iraq.

Figure 215: Protesters rally against the Iraq War, reflecting the growing national division that followed Bush's once-unifying post-9/11 leadership.

But Bush's struggles with Iraq shouldn't overshadow his remarkable achievement in providing effective leadership during the immediate aftermath of September 11. His ability to unite the country, build international coalitions, and articulate a clear response to unprecedented attacks demonstrated leadership capabilities that few observers had recognized before the crisis.

More importantly, Bush's evolution from uncertain politician to confident crisis leader illustrated the unpredictable nature of presidential leadership. The qualities that make someone effective as president often emerge only when they are tested by circumstances that no amount of preparation can anticipate.

Bush's presidency reminds us that leadership is not just about preparation, experience, or intellectual capabilities; it's about the capacity to grow into responsibilities that exceed your previous experience and to find within yourself the strength to make difficult decisions under extreme pressure.

THE UNEXPECTED LEGACY

Figure 216: Bush speaking at the 9/11 Memorial, reflecting his lasting connection to the tragedy that defined his presidency.

Twenty years after September 11, George W. Bush's presidency is remembered primarily for the Iraq War and the controversial policies that followed from his response to terrorism. But his leadership during the immediate crisis deserves recognition as one of American history's most effective examples of presidential crisis management.

Bush's ability to provide emotional leadership while managing complex military and diplomatic responses demonstrated that presidential effectiveness often depends more on character and judgment than on experience or intellectual sophistication. His performance after September 11 proved that leadership capabilities can emerge when circumstances demand them, even in people who comparable challenges have never tested.

Perhaps most importantly, Bush's post-9/11 leadership demonstrated the importance of presidential authenticity during national crises. His most effective moments came when he spoke from the heart rather than from prepared scripts, when he expressed genuine emotion rather than political calculation, and when he connected personally with Americans who were struggling to understand what had happened to their country.

Figure 217: Bush comforting families of 9/11 victims, showing the human cost behind his presidency's defining crisis.

Bush's example reminds us that effective crisis leadership requires the ability to find within yourself capabilities that you may not have known you possessed. The president who was dismissed as unprepared and inexperienced proved that leadership often emerges only when it is desperately needed.

His presidency also illustrates the temporary nature of crisis leadership effectiveness. The qualities that made Bush successful immediately after September 11 proved inadequate for the long-term challenges of governing during wartime. Effective crisis leadership requires not just an initial decisive response but also the flexibility to adapt as circumstances change.

Most importantly, Bush's transformation from uncertain politician to confident crisis leader demonstrates that American democracy's strength lies partly in its ability to call forth leadership from unexpected sources. The president nobody expected to lead became the leader America needed during its moment of greatest vulnerability since Pearl Harbor.

THE CRISIS THAT REVEALS CHARACTER

Figure 218: Bush throws the first pitch at Yankee Stadium in October 2001, symbolizing resilience and unity in the wake of 9/11.

George W. Bush's response to September 11 proved that presidential leadership during a crisis isn't just about policy decisions or strategic planning; it's about the capacity to provide the emotional and symbolic leadership that helps entire nations process trauma and find meaning in tragedy.

Bush's most effective moments as president came when he served as the nation's voice during a period when Americans couldn't find words for what they had experienced. His ability to express collective grief, anger, and determination gave Americans a framework for understanding their own emotions and a sense of direction for moving forward.

This kind of emotional leadership requires personal qualities that can't be taught or learned through experience, authenticity, empathy, and the ability to find exactly the right words at exactly the right moment. Bush discovered these capabilities within himself only when circumstances forced him to reach deeper than he had ever reached before.

Figure 219: Americans waving flags and holding unity signs after 9/11, reflecting the nationwide support sparked by Bush's leadership.

Bush's presidency reminds us that democracy's greatest strength may be its ability to produce leaders who can rise to occasions that exceed their previous experience. The attacks of September 11 called forth leadership capabilities in Bush that might never have emerged under normal circumstances.

His example suggests that effective presidential leadership isn't just about qualifications or experience; it's about character traits that become visible only when tested by extraordinary circumstances. The president who had been dismissed as intellectually lightweight proved that wisdom often emerges from moral clarity rather than analytical sophistication.

Most importantly, Bush's response to September 11 demonstrated that American democracy can produce leaders who are capable of growth, adaptation, and transformation when their country needs them most. The man who became president almost by accident became the leader America needed during its darkest hour since World War II.

George W. Bush's leadership after September 11 illustrates how presidential effectiveness often depends more on character and authenticity than on experience or intellectual sophistication. His transformation from uncertain politician to confident crisis leader demonstrated that leadership capabilities can emerge when circumstances demand them, even in people who comparable challenges have never tested. Bush's ability to provide emotional and symbolic leadership while managing complex crisis responses proved that effective presidential leadership requires not just policy expertise but also the capacity to help entire nations process trauma and find direction during periods of unprecedented challenge. His presidency reminds us that American democracy's strength lies partly in its ability to call forth leadership from unexpected sources, and that the qualities that make someone effective as president often become visible only when tested by extraordinary circumstances. While Bush's later struggles with Iraq revealed the limitations of his leadership style, his response to September 11 remains one of the most effective examples of presidential crisis management in American history.

Part IV:

The Hidden Truth About American Courage

Chapter 12:
What Makes a Hero?

THE ANATOMY OF COURAGE IN CRISIS

Figure 220: A collection of American heroes, representing the diverse faces of strength and determination throughout history.

What connects a disabled spy who outsmarted the Gestapo, an enslaved man who risked everything for a country that enslaved him, a teenage girl who rode through enemy territory, a formerly enslaved seamstress who counseled presidents, a gay organizer who orchestrated the March on Washington, and a woman who taught leaders how to lead?

After following these remarkable Americans through their moments of crisis and courage, we can finally answer the question that has haunted American history since its beginning: What makes someone a hero? And perhaps more importantly: Why do we remember some heroes while forgetting others?

The answer isn't what most of us learned in school. American heroism isn't about perfect people making perfect decisions during moments of obvious crisis. It's about ordinary people making extraordinary choices when the stakes are highest and the outcome is most uncertain. It's about individuals who refuse to accept that "someone else" will solve the problem, step forward when it is dangerous, and sacrifice personal safety for the collective good.

Figure 221: A montage of American heroism in action, showing pivotal crisis moments from the Pyrenees crossing

But our exploration of hidden patriots reveals something even more profound about American courage: the people who shape history most decisively are often those who society overlooks, underestimates, or deliberately ignores. The real builders of American democracy have consistently been women in a man's world, minorities in a white majority, the disabled in an ableist society, and the marginalized fighting for a mainstream that rejects them.

This pattern isn't accidental. It reveals fundamental truths about how courage develops, how democracy functions, and why some people step forward when others step back. Understanding these patterns can help us recognize the hidden heroes among us today, and perhaps become heroes ourselves when our moment comes.

THE OUTSIDER'S ADVANTAGE

Figure 222: Virginia Hall using her wooden leg "Cuthbert" to navigate difficult terrain

Every hero in our story shared a crucial characteristic: they were outsiders who society had written off or underestimated. The State Department rejected Virginia Hall because her disability supposedly made her unsuitable for the foreign service. James Armistead Lafayette was an enslaved person who wasn't supposed to possess the intelligence needed for complex strategic thinking. Sybil Ludington was a teenage girl in an era when women were considered incapable of military contributions.

This outsider status wasn't a coincidence but a crucial factor in their heroic achievements. Being underestimated gave them operational advantages that more obvious candidates for heroism couldn't possess. Virginia Hall's disability made her invisible to Nazi security services, who couldn't imagine that a limping woman could be conducting sophisticated espionage operations. James Armistead Lafayette's enslaved status allowed him to move freely between American and British forces without arousing suspicion.

But the outsider's advantage went deeper than tactical considerations. These individuals had been forced to develop capabilities that privileged people never needed to acquire. Virginia Hall's experience with disability had taught her to solve problems creatively and persist through obstacles that would have defeated most people. Elizabeth Keckley's journey from slavery to freedom had developed her psychological resilience and strategic thinking.

Figure 223: Elizabeth Keckley in the White House, showing how her outsider perspective provided unique insights to the Lincoln administration.

Most importantly, their outsider status gave them clarity about what was worth fighting for. They understood the gap between American ideals and American reality because they had experienced that gap personally. They fought hardest for democracy because they knew what it felt like to be denied democratic rights. They served most faithfully because they understood most clearly what was at stake.

This pattern challenges fundamental assumptions about heroism and capability that continue to influence American society today. We tend to look for heroes among people who already possess obvious qualifications, military experience, political connections, educational credentials, and social status. But our hidden patriots prove that the most effective heroes are often those who have been systematically excluded from positions of obvious authority.

Their example suggests that American society consistently wastes human potential by underestimating people based on their race, gender, disability, sexual orientation, or social background. The people we dismiss as incapable of heroism may be exactly the people whose unique perspectives and experiences make them most capable of extraordinary achievement.

THE COURAGE OF THE UNDERESTIMATED

Figure 224: Bayard Rustin, the logistical mastermind of the March on Washington, worked in the background to ensure the historic event's success.

Traditional definitions of courage focus on physical bravery, soldiers charging into battle, firefighters rushing into burning buildings, and police officers confronting dangerous criminals. But the heroes in our story demonstrate that the most important courage is often moral rather than physical, requiring the strength to do the right thing when it's personally costly rather than the strength to overcome physical obstacles.

Virginia Hall's courage wasn't just about surviving behind enemy lines but about volunteering for dangerous missions when she could have chosen safety. James Armistead Lafayette's courage wasn't just about risking capture as a spy; it was about serving a country that kept him enslaved. Bayard Rustin's courage wasn't just about organizing dangerous civil rights demonstrations; it was about accepting invisibility so the movement could succeed.

This moral courage requires qualities that can't be taught in military academies or leadership seminars: the ability to maintain hope when success seems impossible, the willingness to sacrifice personal recognition for collective achievement, and the capacity to keep working when the benefits of that work might not be realized for generations.

Figure 225: Illustrate a small, intimate meeting in the 1960s where civil rights activist Ella Baker is guiding and empowering a diverse group of young activists

Perhaps most remarkably, these heroes demonstrated courage not just in dramatic moments but in the patient, sustained work that made dramatic moments possible. Ella Baker's heroism wasn't just about attending dangerous meetings in the segregated South but about spending decades developing grassroots leadership that could sustain social movements over time. Elizabeth Keckley's heroism wasn't just about comforting Mary Lincoln during her husband's assassination; it was about years of quiet influence that helped hold the Lincoln administration together during the Civil War.

This sustained moral courage may be more important than dramatic physical bravery for the functioning of democratic societies. Democracy depends on citizens who are willing to do the unglamorous work of building institutions, developing leadership, and maintaining civic engagement even when the immediate benefits aren't obvious.

The heroes in our story prove that this kind of sustained moral courage is available to ordinary people who choose to develop it. None of them started out as obviously heroic figures; they became heroes through decisions they made about how to respond to the challenges they faced.

THE POWER OF REFUSING TO ACCEPT "NO"

Figure 2.26: Sybil Ludington mounting her horse, Star, a crucial moment when she decided to act despite obstacles.

Every hero in our story reached a moment when conventional wisdom, social expectations, or practical limitations suggested they should step back and let someone else handle the problem. Virginia Hall was told her disability made her unsuitable for foreign service. James Armistead Lafayette lived in a society that considered enslaved people incapable of strategic thinking. Sybil Ludington was a teenage girl in an era when women weren't supposed to undertake military missions.

But heroism begins with rejecting other people's limitations and acting based on your own assessment of what's possible and necessary. These individuals refused to accept that their gender, race, age, disability, or social status disqualified them from making crucial contributions to their country's welfare.

This refusal to accept "no" required more than just stubbornness or ego; it required the ability to see possibilities that others missed and the confidence to act on those insights despite social pressure to conform. Virginia Hall understood that her disability could be an asset rather than a liability in espionage work. Ella Baker recognized that grassroots organizing could be more effective than charismatic leadership in building sustainable social movements.

Figure 227: Ella Baker's vision of participatory leadership challenged conventional assumptions

Most importantly, these heroes understood that waiting for permission or social approval would mean that crucial work simply wouldn't get done. They stepped forward not because they were seeking glory or recognition, but because they could see that someone needed to take responsibility and was willing to be that person.

This pattern reveals something crucial about how social progress happens in democratic societies. Change doesn't come from established institutions or recognized authorities deciding to reform themselves; it comes from individuals who refuse to accept unjust or ineffective systems and are willing to risk their personal security to create alternatives.

The heroes in our story didn't wait for society to recognize their capabilities or grant them permission to act. They simply began doing the work that needed to be done and proved through their achievements that society's assumptions about their limitations were wrong.

THE HIDDEN NETWORKS OF HEROISM

Figure 228: A stylized network diagram showing the connections between different heroes

One of the most important discoveries from studying hidden patriots is that heroism is rarely a solo performance. Even the most independent heroes in our story succeeded because they were able to build networks of relationships with other people who shared their commitment to important causes.

Virginia Hall's espionage networks included hundreds of French resistance fighters, British SOE officers, and American OSS operatives who provided intelligence, logistical support, and protection that made her missions possible. Ella Baker's influence on the civil rights movement came through her ability to identify and develop leadership capacity in thousands of young activists who carried her organizing philosophy into communities across the South.

These networks weren't just tactical necessities; they were manifestations of the democratic values that the heroes were fighting to protect. By working collaboratively rather than seeking individual glory, they were demonstrating that democratic societies function best when they develop the capabilities of many people rather than depending on the genius of a few exceptional individuals.

Figure 229: Collective heroism was a powerful force during World War II

The collaborative nature of heroism also reveals why some heroes remain hidden while others become famous. The people who seek individual recognition and credit often receive it, while those who focus on developing others' capabilities and building sustainable institutions remain largely invisible to history.

This pattern suggests that the most important heroes may be those we never hear about, the individuals who spend their lives creating conditions that allow other people to achieve visible success. Ella Baker's philosophy that "the movement made Martin, not Martin the movement" applies to countless hidden patriots who have shaped American history without receiving recognition for their contributions.

Understanding heroism as a collaborative rather than individual phenomenon has important implications for how we think about developing courage and leadership in contemporary society. Instead of looking for exceptional individuals who can solve problems single-handedly, we should focus on building networks and institutions that can develop and support many people's capacity for heroic action.

THE TEST OF TIME

Figure 230: The continuing influence of Ella Baker's model of participatory leadership

The ultimate test of heroism isn't whether someone performs courageously in a moment of crisis; it's whether their actions create lasting positive change that continues to benefit society long after their individual contribution is complete. By this standard, the hidden patriots in our story were remarkably successful heroes whose achievements continue to influence American society today.

Virginia Hall's pioneering work in intelligence operations helped establish the CIA and influenced modern approaches to espionage that continue to protect American security. The organizational methods that Ella Baker developed for civil rights work have been adapted by environmental, immigrant rights, and economic justice movements that are addressing contemporary challenges.

But perhaps more importantly, these heroes established precedents that expanded American understanding of who could contribute to democratic governance and social progress. James Armistead Lafayette's success as a spy helped prove that enslaved people possessed intelligence and loyalty that slavery was designed to suppress. Bayard Rustin's organizational genius demonstrated that sexual minorities could make crucial contributions to social justice movements.

Figure 231: The 2008 election of Barack Obama, representing how the heroes' work expanded possibilities for leadership

The long-term impact of their heroism can be seen in contemporary American society, where women serve as intelligence officers, African Americans hold the highest elected offices, and LGBTQ+ individuals occupy positions of leadership that were unimaginable during the heroes' lifetimes. Their individual acts of courage helped create a society where heroism is more widely distributed and more broadly recognized.

This suggests that true heroism involves not just solving immediate problems but also creating new possibilities for future generations. The most effective heroes are those who use their individual achievements to challenge systematic limitations and expand society's understanding of human potential.

The heroes in our story succeeded not just in accomplishing their immediate goals but in proving that American democracy could be stronger and more inclusive than its founders had originally envisioned. Their courage helped create the America we live in today.

THE MODERN RECOGNITION PROBLEM

Figure 232: A contemporary memorial or statue honoring previously overlooked heroes

One of the most troubling patterns revealed by studying hidden patriots is how long it often takes for American society to recognize and honor the contributions of its most important heroes. Virginia Hall didn't receive significant public recognition until decades after her death. Bayard Rustin was largely ignored by mainstream histories of the civil rights movement until the 1980s. James Armistead Lafayette remains unknown to most Americans despite his crucial role in securing independence.

This delayed recognition isn't just a historical curiosity; it reflects ongoing problems with how American society identifies and celebrates heroism. We tend to honor people who fit comfortable stereotypes about what heroes should look like, while overlooking those whose achievements challenge our assumptions about capability and contribution.

The result is that we continue to waste human potential by underestimating people based on characteristics that have nothing to do with their capacity for extraordinary achievement. Contemporary society may be overlooking heroes whose contributions could address current challenges, simply because they don't fit traditional expectations about leadership and capability.

Figure 233: Modern unsung heroes; healthcare workers, teachers, and community organizers

More importantly, delayed recognition means that society loses opportunities to learn from heroes' examples and apply their insights to contemporary challenges. Civil rights organizations might have been more effective if we had understood Ella Baker's organizing philosophy during her lifetime. If Virginia Hall's achievements had been publicized during World War II, it might have accelerated opportunities for women in intelligence work.

The pattern of delayed recognition suggests that American society needs better methods for identifying and supporting heroic contributions while they're happening, rather than waiting for historians to discover them decades later. This requires developing an appreciation for different forms of courage and achievement, particularly those that work behind the scenes or challenge conventional assumptions.

It also requires recognizing that the people making the most important contributions to contemporary society may be those who seem least likely to be heroes, the outsiders, the underestimated, the individuals who are working quietly to solve problems that established institutions haven't been able to address.

HEROISM IN THE AGE OF SOCIAL MEDIA

Figure 234: Contemporary activists organize through social media platforms

Understanding historical patterns of heroism has particular relevance in our current era, when social media and instant communication have transformed how courage is displayed and recognized. Unlike the hidden patriots of previous generations, contemporary heroes often have opportunities for immediate recognition and broad visibility that can amplify their impact but also create new challenges.

The democratic organizing methods that Ella Baker pioneered are now being adapted by movements that use social media to build grassroots networks and develop distributed leadership. The kind of behind-the-scenes coordination that Bayard Rustin mastered for the March on Washington can now be accomplished through digital tools that allow real-time communication between organizers across great distances.

But modern technology also creates new pressures that can interfere with the development of authentic heroism. The constant possibility of publicity can encourage people to focus on activities that will generate social media attention rather than doing the patient, unglamorous work that creates lasting change.

Figure 235: A split screen showing historical organizing meetings versus contemporary digital organizing

Perhaps more importantly, modern communication's speed can prevent the sustained, thoughtful organizing that characterized the most effective historical heroes. Ella Baker spent decades developing the relationships and institutions that made the civil rights movement successful. Contemporary movements often focus on immediate responses to current events rather than building the long-term capacity needed for systematic change.

The heroes in our story offer important lessons for navigating these modern challenges. Their emphasis on developing others' leadership rather than seeking personal recognition provides a model for using social media tools to build movements rather than personal brands. Their focus on creating lasting institutions rather than winning immediate victories suggests that contemporary heroes need to balance urgent response with patient organizing.

Most importantly, their example reminds us that true heroism often requires stepping away from the spotlight and doing work that may not receive immediate recognition but that creates foundations for future progress.

THE DEMOCRACY WE DESERVE

Figure 236: A diverse group of contemporary Americans, engaged in civic activities

The hidden patriots in our story didn't just serve their country during moments of crisis; they helped create a democracy that was more inclusive, more effective, and more true to its founding ideals than the one they inherited. Their heroism expanded American understanding of who could contribute to democratic governance and how citizen participation could address seemingly impossible challenges.

Virginia Hall and the other women who served in intelligence roles during World War II proved that effective national security required utilizing the talents of all citizens rather than limiting crucial work to traditional demographic groups. James Armistead Lafayette's success as a spy challenged fundamental assumptions about racial capability that had been used to justify slavery and exclusion.

Ella Baker's organizing philosophy demonstrated that democracy worked best when it developed the leadership capacity of entire communities rather than depending on charismatic individuals or established institutions. Her methods provided templates for grassroots organizing that continue to influence contemporary social movements.

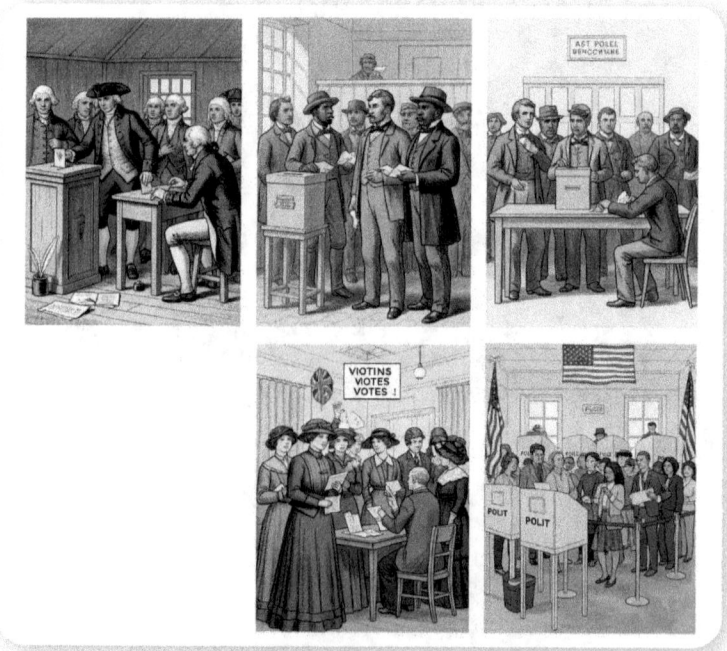

Figure 237: The evolution of American democracy

But perhaps most importantly, these heroes proved that American ideals of equality and opportunity were achievable goals rather than impossible dreams. By demonstrating capabilities that society claimed they couldn't possess and achieving successes that conventional wisdom said were impossible, they expanded American understanding of human potential and democratic possibility.

Their example suggests that contemporary American democracy continues to waste human potential by underestimating people based on characteristics that have nothing to do with their capacity for contribution. The current challenges facing American society, climate change, inequality, political polarization, and international competition may require heroic contributions from people who don't fit traditional expectations about leadership and capability.

The hidden patriots of American history remind us that democracy's greatest strength may be its ability to call forth heroism from unexpected sources when circumstances require extraordinary responses to unprecedented challenges.

THE CALL TO HIDDEN HEROISM

Figure 238: A composite of a teacher, a community organizer, and a citizen, representing the modern opportunities for heroic action.

The most important lesson from studying America's hidden patriots isn't that heroism belongs to exceptional people in exceptional times; it's that opportunities for heroic action exist in every generation for anyone willing to recognize and seize them. The qualities that made Virginia Hall, James Armistead Lafayette, Sybil Ludington, Elizabeth Keckley, Bayard Rustin, and Ella Baker heroic are available to contemporary Americans who choose to develop them.

Heroism begins with the recognition that someone needs to take responsibility for solving problems that established institutions haven't been able to address. It requires the courage to step forward when stepping forward is personally costly and the outcome is uncertain. It demands the patience to do sustained work that may not produce immediate results or recognition.

Most importantly, heroism requires the humility to focus on creating conditions for other people's success rather than seeking personal glory or recognition. The most effective heroes are often those who make other people more capable and confident rather than those who demonstrate their own exceptional abilities.

Figure 239: A person reading a book, perhaps making notes or looking thoughtfully into the distance

Contemporary America faces challenges that require exactly the kind of heroic response that the hidden patriots of previous generations provided. Climate change, economic inequality, political polarization, and technological disruption create opportunities for individuals who are willing to step forward and do the difficult work of building solutions that established institutions haven't been able to develop.

The people who will address these challenges may not look like traditional heroes; they may be young people who are dismissed as inexperienced, women who are underestimated because of their gender, minorities who are overlooked because of their race, or individuals with disabilities who are assumed to be incapable of significant contribution.

But suppose the pattern of American heroism continues. In that case, the solutions to contemporary challenges will come from exactly these unexpected sources, from the outsiders who refuse to accept limitations, from the underestimated who understand what's at stake, from the hidden patriots who are willing to do whatever work is necessary to protect and strengthen American democracy.

The question isn't whether heroic opportunities exist in contemporary America; they're everywhere around us. The question is whether we have the courage to recognize them and commit to acting on them, even when acting requires sacrificing our comfort, security, or certainty about how the story will end.

The hidden patriots of American history proved that ordinary people can achieve extraordinary things when they're willing to step forward and serve something larger than themselves. Their example reminds us that the next generation of American heroes may be reading these words right now, wondering whether they have what it takes to make a difference.

The answer is: you probably do. The question is: what are you going to do about it?

The hidden patriots of American history reveal that heroism isn't about perfect people making perfect decisions during obvious crises; it's about ordinary individuals choosing to act courageously when the stakes are highest and the outcome is most uncertain. These unsung heroes shared crucial characteristics: they were outsiders who society had underestimated, they possessed moral courage that sustained them through long periods of unglamorous work, they refused to accept other people's limitations on their potential, and they focused on creating lasting change rather than seeking immediate recognition. Their achievements expanded American democracy and proved that the people who serve their country most faithfully are often those who have the most reason to question whether their country deserves their service. Understanding their patterns of heroism can help us recognize the hidden patriots among us today and perhaps discover the heroic potential within ourselves. In every generation, American democracy depends on individuals who are willing to step forward when stepping forward is difficult, to serve something larger than themselves, and to prove through their actions that the ideals of freedom and equality are worth defending.

Chapter 13:
The Heroes Among Us

FINDING SECRET PATRIOTS IN MODERN AMERICA

Figure 240: Modern unsung heroes, including a teacher, a community organizer, a whistleblower, and a food bank volunteer, represent the hidden patriots of today.

On a cold Tuesday morning in December 2019, Dr. Li Wenliang, an ophthalmologist in Wuhan, China, sent a message to his medical school classmates warning them about a cluster of unusual pneumonia cases he had observed. His message included a simple but prophetic warning: "7 confirmed cases of SARS were reported from Huanan Seafood Market." He asked his colleagues to be careful and protect their families.

Dr. Li was wrong about one detail: it wasn't SARS, but a novel coronavirus that would soon be known as COVID-19. But his instinct to warn others, despite having no official authority to issue public health alerts, represented exactly the kind of courageous individual action that has always characterized America's hidden patriots.

Within days, Chinese authorities had forced Dr. Li to sign a statement acknowledging that his warning constituted "illegal behavior." A month later, he contracted the virus. At the same time, treating patients and died at age 34, becoming a symbol of the individual courage required to speak truth to power when institutions fail to protect public welfare.

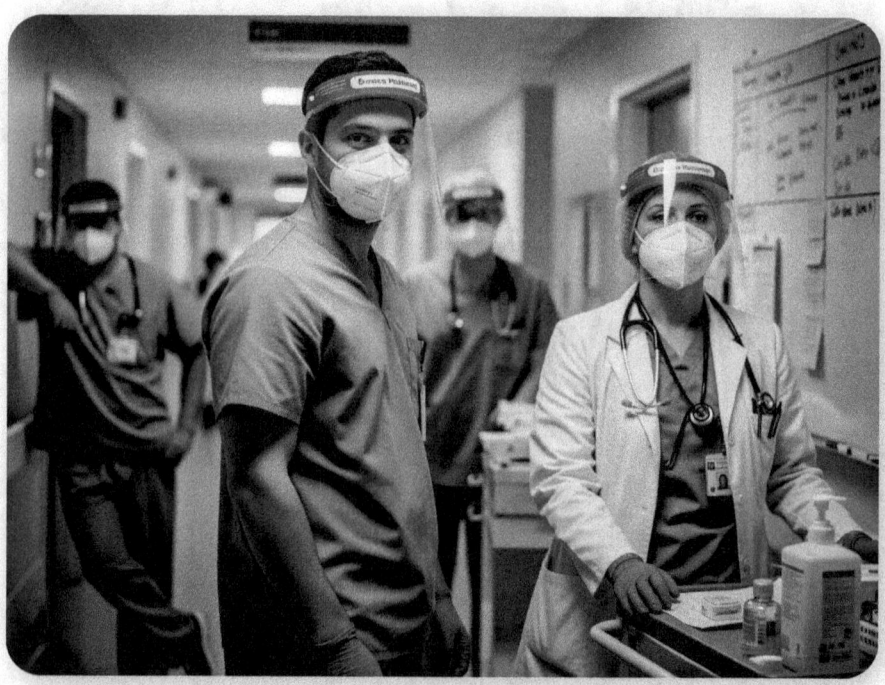

Figure 241: Healthcare workers on the front lines of the COVID-19 pandemic

Dr. Li's story reminds us that the same patterns of hidden heroism that shaped American history continue to emerge today, often in the most ordinary circumstances and among the most unexpected people. The nurse who speaks up about unsafe working conditions, the teacher who uses her own money to buy supplies for students, the community organizer who builds bridges between divided neighborhoods, these contemporary Americans are following in the footsteps of Virginia Hall, Ella Baker, and Bayard Rustin.

But recognizing modern heroes requires understanding what heroism looks like in the 21st century, when the challenges facing democracy are different but no less urgent than those confronted by previous generations. Climate change, economic inequality, political polarization, and technological disruption create new opportunities for the kind of individual courage and collective action that have always driven American progress.

The secret patriots of today may not be breaking enemy codes or organizing freedom rides. Still, they are doing equally important work: developing renewable energy technologies, fighting for criminal justice reform, protecting voting rights, providing healthcare during a pandemic, and building the institutions that will determine whether American democracy survives its current challenges.

THE DIGITAL UNDERGROUND RAILROAD

Figure 242: Computer screens showing online organizing platforms, encrypted communications

In the summer of 2020, as protests against police brutality spread across the country, a network of technology workers began quietly using their skills to support demonstrators who were facing police surveillance and digital tracking. These programmers, cybersecurity experts, and data scientists weren't marching in the streets or giving speeches at rallies; they were working behind the scenes to protect protesters' privacy and safety.

Some developed encrypted messaging apps that allowed organizers to communicate without government surveillance. Others created digital security training programs that taught activists how to protect their phones and computers from law enforcement monitoring. Still others used their access to corporate databases to expose police misconduct and document patterns of abuse that traditional journalism couldn't uncover.

These technology workers were following a pattern established by previous generations of hidden patriots: using their specialized skills to serve causes larger than their personal interests, often at significant professional and legal risk. Like the women codebreakers of World War II, they understood that democracy depends on citizens who are willing to use their expertise to protect constitutional rights and democratic institutions.

Figure 243: A diverse group of programmers and tech workers in a late-night coding session, developing tools for social justice movements.

But the digital underground railroad represents more than just technical support for political movements; it illustrates how contemporary heroism often requires adapting traditional values to new circumstances. The fundamental commitment to justice and equality that motivated historical civil rights activists remains the same. Still, the methods for advancing those values must evolve to address the realities of surveillance capitalism and digital authoritarianism.

Modern secret patriots in the technology sector understand that protecting democracy in the 21st century requires not just defending traditional civil liberties but also creating new forms of digital rights and protections. They are working to ensure that emerging technologies serve democratic values rather than undermining them, often in direct opposition to the corporate and governmental institutions that employ them.

The programmers who risk their careers to expose surveillance abuses, the engineers who design privacy-protecting technologies, and the data scientists who document systemic inequalities are continuing the work that James Armistead Lafayette began when he used his intelligence skills to serve freedom rather than oppression.

Their example reminds us that every generation of Americans must figure out how to apply timeless values to contemporary challenges, and that heroism often requires mastering new tools while maintaining old commitments.

THE CLIMATE CASSANDRAS

Figure 244: A young climate scientist presents data to skeptical policymakers, representing the courage required to persist with unwelcome truths.

Dr. Kathryn Hayhoe has spent two decades trying to convince Americans that climate change poses an existential threat to their communities, economy, and way of life. As an atmospheric scientist and professor at Texas Tech University, she has published hundreds of peer-reviewed papers documenting how rising temperatures are already affecting American agriculture, infrastructure, and public health.

But Dr. Hayhoe's heroism isn't just about scientific research; it's about her willingness to persist in communicating urgent truths to audiences who often don't want to hear them. As an evangelical Christian working in conservative Texas, she faces constant personal attacks and professional pressure for insisting that climate change is real and requires immediate action.

Like the hidden patriots of previous generations, Dr. Hayhoe understands that effective heroism often requires finding ways to communicate across ideological divisions and build coalitions that transcend traditional political boundaries. She frames climate action in terms of stewardship and protection of future generations rather than using the partisan language that has made environmental issues politically toxic.

Figure 245: Solar panels being installed on a working farm, representing practical solutions that bridge ideological divides.

Dr. Hayhoe is part of a broader network of climate scientists, activists, and policy experts working to address the greatest challenge in human history. Like Ella Baker's approach to civil rights organizing, their strategy emphasizes grassroots education and local action rather than depending entirely on federal policy changes or international agreements.

These modern environmental patriots include the farmers who are adopting regenerative agriculture practices that rebuild soil and sequester carbon, the engineers who are developing renewable energy technologies that can compete economically with fossil fuels, and the community organizers who are building political coalitions that can sustain climate action over decades.

Perhaps most importantly, they include the young activists who are willing to disrupt their own education and career prospects to demand that adults take climate change seriously. Like Sybil Ludington riding through the night to rally colonial militia, these young people understand that their generation's future depends on their willingness to take actions that previous generations have been unwilling or unable to take.

The climate movement's emphasis on intergenerational justice and long-term thinking reflects the same moral clarity that motivated historical heroes who fought for principles that wouldn't be fully realized in their own lifetimes. These contemporary patriots are willing to sacrifice immediate comfort and security for the possibility that future generations will inherit a livable planet.

THE DEMOCRACY DEFENDERS

Figure 246: Election workers counting ballots under intense scrutiny, representing the civic heroes who maintain democratic processes despite political pressure.

On January 6, 2021, as rioters stormed the U.S. Capitol trying to overturn the results of the presidential election, a handful of election officials across the country were quietly documenting the threats and pressure they had faced for months while trying to conduct fair and accurate elections.

In Georgia, Secretary of State Brad Raffensperger had withstood intense pressure from his own party to "find" votes that would change the election outcome. In Arizona, Maricopa County election officials had faced death threats for refusing to alter vote counts. In Michigan, local election workers had required police protection while counting ballots.

These election officials weren't famous politicians or movement leaders; they were mostly career civil servants who understood that democracy depends on the integrity of basic administrative processes. Like Elizabeth Keckley, who provided stability to the Lincoln White House during the Civil War, they maintained essential democratic

Figure 247: A small-town election official working alone in a courthouse, representing the quiet dedication that maintains democratic institutions.

But the democracy defenders include more than just election officials. They include the journalists who investigate corruption despite threats and harassment, the judges who make decisions based on law rather than political pressure, and the civil servants who continue to serve the public interest even when their agencies are under political attack.

Perhaps most importantly, they include the ordinary citizens who participate in democratic processes despite the time, effort, and sometimes personal risk that participation requires. The voters who wait in long lines during voter suppression attempts, the citizens who attend local government meetings to advocate for their communities, and the volunteers who register voters and provide civic education are all continuing the work that Ella Baker described as essential to democratic functioning.

These contemporary patriots understand that democracy isn't a self-maintaining system; it requires constant care and protection by people who value democratic institutions more than their own comfort or convenience. Like the hidden patriots of previous generations, they are willing to sacrifice their time, energy, and sometimes their safety to preserve the democratic rights that future generations will depend on.

Their work reminds us that heroism in a democratic society often consists of protecting boring but essential processes rather than engaging in dramatic confrontations. The election worker who stays late to ensure accurate vote counts, the local government official who insists on transparency despite political pressure, and the citizen who shows up to city council meetings are all performing acts of civic heroism that keep democracy functioning.

THE HEALING PROFESSIONALS

Figure 248: A rural doctor making house calls during the pandemic, representing healthcare workers who serve underserved communities despite personal risk.

Dr. Ala Stanford was working as a pediatric surgeon in Philadelphia when the COVID-19 pandemic revealed massive disparities in healthcare access that were leaving Black and Latino communities without adequate testing and treatment. Instead of waiting for government agencies or healthcare institutions to address these disparities, Dr. Stanford created her own mobile testing operation that brought COVID tests directly to underserved neighborhoods.

Working out of her car and using her own money, Dr. Stanford and a growing network of volunteer healthcare workers conducted thousands of tests in communities that the formal healthcare system had ignored. When vaccines became available, she expanded her operation to provide mobile vaccination clinics that could reach people who lacked transportation or couldn't take time off work to visit traditional healthcare facilities.

Dr. Stanford's work during the pandemic illustrates a pattern of contemporary heroism that extends far beyond healthcare: professionals using their expertise to serve communities that institutions have failed to reach. Like Virginia Hall using her skills to serve a cause larger than her own advancement, these modern patriots are applying their training and resources to address systematic inequalities rather than just building their own careers.

Figure 249: A mobile vaccination clinic in an underserved neighborhood, showing healthcare workers providing services where they're most needed.

The healing professionals include more than just doctors and nurses. They include the mental health counselors who provide therapy to trauma survivors, the social workers who help families navigate complex bureaucratic systems, and the community health workers who provide education and support in neighborhoods that lack access to formal healthcare services.

Perhaps most importantly, they include the teachers who continue to educate students despite inadequate resources and political attacks on public education. These educators understand that democracy depends on an informed citizenry, and they are willing to use their own money, time, and creativity to ensure that their students receive the education they need to participate effectively in a democratic society.

Like the women who worked as codebreakers during World War II, these contemporary heroes often labor in obscurity while performing work that is essential to national security and democratic functioning. The teacher who stays after school to tutor struggling students, the librarian who helps community members access information and services, and the healthcare worker who provides care regardless of patients' ability to pay are all contributing to the social infrastructure that makes a democratic society possible.

Their example reminds us that heroism often consists of doing essential work excellently rather than seeking recognition or advancement. These modern patriots understand that serving others requires not just good intentions but also professional competence and sustained commitment to excellence in whatever field they have chosen to serve.

THE BRIDGE BUILDERS

Figure 250; A diverse group of people working together on a community project

In rural Oregon, a former logger named Mike Pihl has spent the last decade trying to heal the economic and cultural divisions that have torn apart his community since the timber industry collapsed. Instead of choosing sides in the political battles between environmentalists and rural workers, Pihl has focused on finding practical projects that can benefit everyone while building relationships across ideological lines.

Pihl's organization, the Rural Organizing Project, brings together farmers, loggers, small business owners, and environmental activists to work on issues like internet access, healthcare, and economic development that affect entire communities regardless of political affiliation. By focusing on shared practical concerns rather than divisive political issues, he has created space for people to rediscover their common interests and shared values.

This kind of bridge-building work requires the same patience and strategic thinking that Ella Baker brought to civil rights organizing. Like Baker, Pihl understands that sustainable social change requires building relationships and developing leadership capacity rather than just winning immediate political victories.

Figure 251: A community meeting with people of different backgrounds listening to each other respectfully

The bridge builders include people working in every kind of community to reduce polarization and increase cooperation across dividing lines. They include the religious leaders who bring together congregations from different faiths to work on community problems, the business leaders who invest in economically distressed areas, and the nonprofit directors who build coalitions around specific issues that affect multiple constituencies.

Perhaps most importantly, they include the ordinary citizens who choose to engage with their neighbors as individuals rather than as representatives of political tribes. The suburban parent who volunteers at an inner-city school, the rural farmer who sells produce to urban communities, and the retiree who mentors young people from different backgrounds are all performing acts of civic heroism that strengthen a democratic society.

These contemporary patriots understand that democracy depends not just on formal political institutions but also on the informal relationships and social connections that allow diverse people to work together effectively. Like James Armistead Lafayette, building intelligence networks that crossed racial and political lines, they are creating the social infrastructure that makes democratic governance possible.

Their work reminds us that heroism often consists of choosing connection over division, even when division might be easier or more emotionally satisfying. In an era of unprecedented political polarization, the people who insist on finding common ground and building collaborative relationships are performing essential patriotic service.

THE TRUTH TELLERS

Figure 252: A whistleblower walking toward a government building or courthouse, representing the courage required to expose wrongdoing despite personal risk.

Reality Winner was a 25-year-old Air Force veteran working as a contractor for the National Security Agency when she discovered evidence that Russian intelligence services had attempted to hack American election systems in 2016. Believing that the American people deserved to know about foreign interference in their democracy, Winner leaked a classified document to a news organization that confirmed Russian election interference.

Winner was arrested within weeks of the leak and eventually sentenced to more than five years in federal prison, the longest sentence ever imposed for leaking classified information to the media. Like the hidden patriots of previous generations, she sacrificed her personal freedom for what she believed was the greater good of democratic accountability and transparency.

Winner's case illustrates the complex moral calculations that contemporary truth tellers must make when institutions fail to protect democratic values. Like Virginia Hall operating behind enemy lines, modern whistleblowers must navigate legal and professional risks that can destroy their lives while trying to serve principles that transcend their personal interests.

Figure 253: Journalists working in a newsroom, representing the professionals who risk their careers to investigate and expose corruption.

The truth tellers include more than just government whistleblowers. They include the journalists who investigate powerful people and institutions despite legal threats and economic pressure, the scientists who publish research that contradicts political orthodoxies, and the citizens who document police misconduct and corporate wrongdoing using their cell phones and social media platforms.

Perhaps most importantly, they include the ordinary people who choose to speak honestly about difficult topics in their communities, workplaces, and families. The employee who reports safety violations, the student who challenges discriminatory policies, and the citizen who asks difficult questions at public meetings are all performing acts of civic heroism that strengthen democratic accountability.

These contemporary patriots understand that democracy depends on the free flow of accurate information and that protecting truth often requires personal courage in the face of powerful interests that benefit from secrecy and deception. Like Bayard Rustin accepting invisibility to serve the civil rights movement, modern truth tellers often sacrifice their own security and comfort to protect democratic institutions and values.

Their example reminds us that heroism sometimes requires choosing uncomfortable truths over comfortable lies, even when truth-telling comes with significant personal costs. In an era of information warfare and institutional distrust, the people who insist on accuracy and honesty are performing an essential service to a democratic society.

HOW TO SPOT A HIDDEN HERO

Figure 254: A person quietly cleaning up a neighborhood park

After studying both historical and contemporary examples of hidden patriotism, certain patterns emerge that can help us recognize heroes who are working among us right now. These modern patriots share characteristics with the hidden heroes of previous generations, but they adapt their service to contemporary challenges and opportunities.

The first sign of potential heroism is competence combined with service orientation. Hidden heroes are typically very good at whatever they do professionally, teaching, healthcare, technology, journalism, and community organizing. However, they use their skills to benefit others rather than just advancing their careers. They are the professionals who consistently go beyond their formal job descriptions to serve their communities and their principles.

The second indicator is sustained commitment rather than a dramatic gesture. Real heroes do important work consistently over long periods, often without recognition or immediate reward. They are the people who show up to meetings, volunteer for difficult assignments, and persist with unglamorous but essential tasks that other people avoid.

Figure 255: A volunteer coordinator working late at night organizing relief efforts, representing the sustained commitment that characterizes true heroism.

The third characteristic is a focus on developing others rather than building personal prominence. Like Ella Baker, contemporary heroes often measure their success by how effectively they help other people become more capable and confident. They are the mentors, teachers, and organizers who create opportunities for others to succeed rather than hoarding those opportunities for themselves.

The fourth sign is a willingness to work across traditional boundaries and build unlikely coalitions. Modern heroes understand that addressing complex challenges requires bringing together people with different perspectives, backgrounds, and skills. They are the bridge builders who can find common ground between divided groups and help diverse coalitions function effectively.

Finally, hidden heroes demonstrate moral courage in addition to whatever professional expertise they possess. They are willing to speak truth to power, challenge unjust systems, and take personal risks when democratic values are threatened. They choose principle over convenience, service over safety, and collective good over individual advancement.

These characteristics can help us identify the hidden heroes who are already working in our communities, schools, workplaces, and institutions. They are the people who make everything else work better, who solve problems that others avoid, and who create opportunities for positive change even when conditions seem impossible.

CELEBRATING UNSUNG CONTRIBUTIONS

Figure 256: A community recognition ceremony honoring local heroes, representing how communities can better acknowledge hidden contributions.

One of the most important lessons from studying hidden patriots is the need to develop better methods for recognizing and supporting heroic contributions while they're happening, rather than waiting for historians to discover them decades later. Contemporary society has opportunities to learn from heroes' examples and amplify their impact if we can appropriately identify and celebrate their work.

This doesn't mean that every hero wants or needs public recognition; many, like Ella Baker, deliberately choose to work behind the scenes and would be less effective if they became public figures. But it does mean that communities, organizations, and institutions should develop systems for identifying and supporting the people who are doing essential work, even when that work doesn't generate immediate publicity or measurable outcomes.

Recognition can take many forms beyond traditional awards and media attention. It can include providing resources and support that help heroes be more effective in their work, creating opportunities for them to share their knowledge and methods with others, and building networks that connect heroes with similar challenges and goals.

Figure 257: A mentorship program or training workshop where experienced community leaders share skills with newcomers,

Perhaps most importantly, celebration should focus on the methods and principles that make heroes effective rather than just honoring their individual achievements. Understanding how Virginia Hall built intelligence networks, how Bayard Rustin organized large-scale demonstrations, and how Ella Baker developed grassroots leadership can help contemporary activists become more effective in their own work.

Communities can also celebrate hidden heroes by creating more opportunities for the kind of service that develops heroic capabilities. Volunteer programs, civic education initiatives, mentorship opportunities, and community organizing projects all provide ways for ordinary people to develop the skills and experience that can prepare them for moments when heroic action is needed.

The goal isn't to create a society of professional heroes but to ensure that when challenges arise that require individual courage and collective action, there are people in every community who have the knowledge, skills, and network connections needed to respond effectively.

THE DEMOCRACY LABS

Figure 258: Young people engaged in civic education

Some of the most important contemporary heroism is happening in the grassroots organizations and community institutions that are developing new methods for strengthening democracy and addressing systemic challenges. These "democracy labs" are experimenting with innovative approaches to voter education, community organizing, conflict resolution, and civic engagement that could reshape how Americans participate in democratic governance.

Organizations like the Kettering Foundation, the National Issues Forums Institute, and hundreds of local civic groups are developing new methods for helping citizens engage constructively with complex policy issues and work together across ideological divisions. These efforts represent contemporary versions of the participatory democracy that Ella Baker advocated during the civil rights movement.

Similarly, groups focused on restorative justice, environmental sustainability, and economic equality are developing alternative approaches to persistent social problems that traditional institutions haven't been able to solve effectively. Like the hidden patriots of previous generations, these contemporary innovators are creating new possibilities rather than just criticizing existing failures.

Figure 259: A citizen's assembly or deliberative democracy session where diverse people work together on policy challenges

Perhaps most importantly, these democracy labs are training new generations of leaders who understand that effective citizenship requires more than just voting and complaining about government. They teach practical skills like meeting facilitation, strategic planning, conflict resolution, and coalition building that enable ordinary people to collectively address community problems.

The teachers, trainers, and organizers who run these programs are performing essential heroic service by developing the civic capacity that democracy requires to function effectively. Like Ella Baker mentoring young civil rights activists, they are multiplying their impact by helping other people become more effective democratic participants.

Their work reminds us that heroism often consists of building institutional capacity and developing others' leadership rather than seeking individual recognition or immediate policy victories. The most effective contemporary patriots may be those who are creating the knowledge, skills, and relationships that will enable future generations to address challenges that we can't yet fully anticipate.

YOUR HEROIC MOMENT

Figure 260: A mirror or reflection, representing the reader's opportunity for self-examination and potential heroic action.

The most important question raised by studying America's hidden patriots isn't whether heroic opportunities exist today; they clearly do. The question is whether ordinary people like yourself have what it takes to recognize those opportunities and act on them when they arise.

The heroes in this book weren't born with special capabilities that made them destined for extraordinary achievement. Virginia Hall became a spy after being rejected by the State Department. James Armistead Lafayette volunteered for dangerous intelligence work while being held as enslaved property. Sybil Ludington rode forty miles through enemy territory because she happened to know the local trails better than anyone else.

They became heroes through decisions they made about how to respond to circumstances they hadn't chosen and couldn't control. They saw problems that needed solving, recognized that they had capabilities that could contribute to solutions, and chose to act despite uncertainty about outcomes and risks to their personal safety.

Figure 260: A composite image showing various contemporary challenges

Contemporary America faces challenges that are just as urgent as those confronted by previous generations of hidden patriots. Climate change threatens the survival of human civilization. Economic inequality undermines democratic institutions. Political polarization prevents collective action on shared problems. Technological disruption eliminates traditional jobs while creating new forms of surveillance and control.

These challenges create opportunities for exactly the kind of individual courage and collective action that have always driven American progress. The solutions will likely come from unexpected sources, from the outsiders who refuse to accept limitations, the underestimated who understand what's at stake, and the hidden patriots willing to do whatever work is necessary to protect and strengthen democratic institutions.

You may be one of those people. You may possess skills, knowledge, relationships, or perspectives that could contribute to addressing contemporary challenges in ways that haven't been tried before. You may be positioned to build bridges between divided communities, to expose wrongdoing that institutions want to hide, to develop innovations that could benefit millions of people, or to organize collective action that could change policy and culture.

The question isn't whether you're qualified to be a hero; the question is whether you're willing to step forward when stepping forward is needed, serve something larger than your immediate interests, and persist with important work even when recognition and success aren't guaranteed.

THE PATTERN CONTINUES

Figure 261: A diverse group of Americans from different generations working together on a community project

American history is the story of ordinary people making extraordinary choices when their country needed them most. From James Armistead Lafayette's decision to spy for a nation that enslaved him to Dr. Li Wenliang's choice to warn colleagues about a dangerous new disease, the pattern of individual courage in service of collective welfare continues across generations and cultures.

The hidden patriots of today are following in the footsteps of their historical predecessors while adapting their methods to contemporary challenges. They are using new technologies to organize for social justice, applying professional expertise to serve underserved communities, building coalitions across traditional dividing lines, and speaking truth to power despite personal risks.

Most importantly, they are proving that the American experiment in democratic self-governance continues to depend on citizens who value their country's ideals more than their own comfort and convenience. They are demonstrating that democracy isn't a completed project but an ongoing effort that requires each generation to renew and expand its commitments to equality, justice, and mutual responsibility.

Figure 262: *The American flag, perhaps slightly worn or weathered, representing the ongoing work required to maintain democratic ideals.*

The hidden patriots of American history remind us that heroism isn't reserved for special people in special times; it's available to anyone who chooses to develop the moral courage, practical skills, and strategic thinking that effective service requires. Their examples provide both inspiration and practical guidance for contemporary Americans who want to contribute to addressing the challenges of our own era.

But perhaps most importantly, their stories remind us that the future of American democracy depends not on elected officials or established institutions but on ordinary citizens who are willing to step forward when stepping forward is difficult, to serve when service is costly, and to prove through their actions that the ideals of freedom and equality are worth defending.

The next chapter of American heroism is being written right now by people who may not yet recognize their own potential for extraordinary contribution. The teacher who stays late to help struggling students, the community organizer who builds bridges between divided neighborhoods, the healthcare worker who provides care to underserved populations, the citizen who speaks truth to power despite personal risk, these contemporary Americans are continuing the work that Virginia Hall, Ella Baker, and Bayard Rustin began.

Their stories remind us that American democracy has always depended on the willingness of ordinary people to do extraordinary things when their country needs them most. The question isn't whether heroic opportunities exist today but whether we have the courage to recognize them and the commitment to act on them.

The hidden patriots of American history proved that the answer to that question can be yes, if we choose to make it so.

The secret patriots of contemporary America continue the tradition of ordinary people making extraordinary contributions to a democratic society. From technology workers protecting digital rights to healthcare professionals serving underserved communities, from climate scientists speaking unwelcome truths to election officials maintaining democratic processes under pressure, today's hidden heroes demonstrate that the patterns of American heroism persist across generations. These modern patriots share key characteristics with their historical predecessors: they use professional expertise to serve others, maintain sustained commitment to important work, focus on developing others rather than seeking personal recognition, build coalitions across traditional boundaries, and demonstrate moral courage when democratic values are threatened. Recognizing and supporting these contemporary heroes requires developing better systems for identifying heroic contributions while they're happening, creating opportunities for civic engagement that develop heroic capabilities, and understanding that democracy depends on citizens who value collective welfare more than personal comfort. The next generation of American heroes may be reading these words right now, and their willingness to step forward when stepping forward is needed will determine whether American democracy continues to fulfill its founding promise of equality and justice for all.

Prologue

Figure 263: A faded photograph showing silhouettes of people working

They saved the world, and you've never heard their names.

This isn't hyperbole or marketing rhetoric. It's a simple historical fact that reveals something deeply troubling about how America remembers its heroes and something profoundly hopeful about the courage that ordinary people can discover within themselves when their country needs them most.

The woman who cracked Japan's most sophisticated military codes, shortening World War II and saving countless lives, died in suburban obscurity. The man who organized the March on Washington, one of the most important demonstrations in American history, couldn't march in the front row because his sexuality made him a political liability. The teenage girl who rode forty miles through enemy territory to rally colonial militia, covering twice the distance of Paul Revere's famous ride, remains unknown to most Americans.

Their stories aren't just inspiring tales of individual courage; they're evidence of a systematic pattern in American history that has profound implications for how we understand leadership, democracy, and the potential for heroic action that exists within each of us.

Figure 264: A modern American flag alongside historical documents, photographs, and artifacts representing the hidden stories this book will reveal.

For too long, American history has been told as the story of famous men making famous decisions during famous moments. We learn about presidents and generals, inventors and industrialists, as if American democracy were built by a small number of exceptional individuals rather than millions of ordinary people making extraordinary choices when circumstances demanded them.

This version of history isn't just incomplete, it's dangerous. It teaches us to wait for someone else to solve our problems, to assume that heroism belongs to people who are fundamentally different from ourselves, and to believe that the most important work happens in marble buildings and executive suites rather than in communities and classrooms and on street corners where democracy actually lives.

The real story of America is messier, more complicated, and far more hopeful than the sanitized version we learned in school. It's the story of a disabled woman who became Nazi Germany's most wanted spy, of an enslaved man who helped win American independence while fighting for his own freedom, of women who broke enemy codes. At the same time, their contributions were erased from official records.

It's the story of people who stepped forward when stepping forward was dangerous, served when service was costly, and proved through their actions that American ideals of equality and justice were worth defending even when America itself wasn't ready to extend those ideals to everyone.

Figure 265: A diverse group of contemporary Americans, representing the potential heroes among us today.

Their stories matter not just because they deserve recognition, though they do, but because understanding how heroism actually works can help us recognize the hidden patriots among us today and perhaps discover the heroic potential within ourselves.

In every generation, Americans have faced moments when democracy itself seemed fragile, when the gap between American ideals and American reality appeared unbridgeable, when ordinary citizens had to choose between comfortable silence and dangerous action. The people who chose action and refused to accept that someone else would solve the problem didn't do it because they were saints, geniuses, or natural-born leaders.

They did it because someone had to.

The question this book poses isn't whether you're worthy of their example. The question is whether you're willing to follow it.

Epilogue: The Real American Story

Figure 266: A sunrise over a diverse American landscape

As I finish writing this book, I'm struck by a simple but profound realization: every single story in these pages could have been lost forever. Virginia Hall's achievements were classified for decades. Bayard Rustin's contributions were deliberately hidden by a movement that needed his skills but feared his sexuality. James Armistead Lafayette's service was nearly forgotten by a nation uncomfortable with acknowledging that enslaved people had fought for the freedom they were denied.

The only reason we know their stories now is because someone, historians, family members, activists, archivists, refused to let their contributions disappear entirely. Someone insisted that their examples mattered, that their sacrifices had meaning, that their courage deserved to be remembered and honored.

But how many other stories have been lost? How many other hidden patriots lived and died without anyone documenting their achievements, preserving their letters, or passing down their examples to future generations? How many potential heroes never got the chance to discover their own capacity for extraordinary action because they lived in times and places where such opportunities weren't available to people like them?

Figure 267: An archive or library with countless boxes and files, representing the vast stores of untold stories that remain to be discovered.

These questions remind us that the heroes in this book represent not just exceptional individuals but entire categories of people whose contributions have been systematically overlooked or deliberately erased from American history. For every Virginia Hall whose story was eventually declassified, there were dozens of other women intelligence officers whose achievements remain classified or forgotten. For every Ella Baker whose organizing philosophy was eventually recognized by scholars, there were hundreds of other grassroots leaders whose methods died with them.

This pattern of historical invisibility continues today. In communities across America, people are doing essential work to address climate change, protect democratic institutions, heal divided communities, and serve marginalized populations. Most of them will never receive recognition for their contributions. Their names won't appear in history books. Their methods won't be studied by academics.

But their work continues the tradition established by the hidden patriots in this book: ordinary people making extraordinary choices when their country needs them most, proving through their actions that democracy depends not on perfect leaders making perfect decisions but on imperfect people refusing to accept imperfect circumstances.

Figure 268: Contemporary Americans engaged in various forms of civic action=

Understanding this tradition has practical implications for how we live our own lives and engage with the challenges facing contemporary America. It means recognizing that the people who will solve today's problems may not look like traditional heroes. They may be young people dismissed as inexperienced, women underestimated because of their gender, minorities overlooked because of their race, or individuals with disabilities assumed to be incapable of significant contribution.

It means developing our own capacity for the kind of sustained moral courage that characterized the heroes in this book, the willingness to persist with important work even when recognition isn't guaranteed, to serve causes larger than our own immediate interests, and to build institutions and relationships that can outlast our individual contributions.

Most importantly, it means understanding that heroism isn't a quality that some people possess and others lack; it's a choice that becomes available to anyone willing to step forward when stepping forward is needed, to speak truth when truth is dangerous, and to serve when service is costly.

Figure 269: A path leading toward the horizon, perhaps through diverse American landscapes, representing the ongoing journey toward a more perfect union.

The heroes in this book proved that American democracy is not a completed project but an ongoing experiment that requires each generation to renew and expand its commitments to equality, justice, and mutual responsibility. They demonstrated that the gap between American ideals and American reality can be closed, but only through the sustained effort of people who refuse to accept that gap as permanent or inevitable.

Their examples remind us that the most patriotic thing Americans can do isn't to pretend that our country has already achieved its founding promises but to work actively to fulfill those promises for people who have been excluded from their benefits. True patriotism requires the courage to criticize what America is while working to create what America could become.

The secret patriots of American history didn't serve their country because it was perfect; they served it because they could help make it better. They understood that democracy's greatest strength isn't that it produces perfect outcomes but that it provides mechanisms for continuous improvement when citizens are willing to do the work that improvement requires.

Figure 270: Children of diverse backgrounds learning together, representing the future that heroic work makes possible.

As you close this book and return to your own life, the question isn't whether heroic opportunities exist in contemporary America; they're everywhere around us. Climate change, economic inequality, political polarization, and technological disruption create challenges that require exactly the kind of individual courage and collective action that have always driven American progress.

The question is whether you're willing to see and act on those opportunities, even when acting requires sacrificing your comfort, security, or certainty about how the story will end.

The hidden patriots of American history offer no guarantees about the outcomes of heroic action. Virginia Hall could have been captured and executed. James Armistead Lafayette could have been discovered and killed as a spy. Bayard Rustin could have been arrested and imprisoned for his organizing work.

But they also offer something more valuable than guarantees: proof that ordinary people can achieve extraordinary things when they're willing to serve something larger than themselves, evidence that American democracy has always depended on citizens who value their country's ideals more than their own immediate interests, and hope that the same courage that built America in the past can strengthen America in the future.

Figure 271: A hand reaching toward a voting booth, a community meeting, a protest sign, or another symbol of civic engagement, representing the reader's opportunity to participate in democracy.

The statue-makers got it wrong. America wasn't built by perfect people making perfect decisions during perfect moments. It was built by flawed humans doing extraordinary things when everything fell apart. It was built by people who refused to accept that someone else would solve the problem, who stepped forward when stepping forward was dangerous, and who proved through their actions that democratic ideals were worth defending even when democracy itself seemed fragile.

This is your inheritance. This is your challenge. This is your opportunity.

The question isn't whether you're worthy of their example. The question is what you're going to do with it.

"Courage is not the absence of fear, but action in spite of it. And in America's darkest hours, ordinary people have always found extraordinary ways to light the path forward."
The story continues with you.

Thank You!

Thank you for reading "The Secret Patriots: Hidden Heroes Who Shaped America When It Mattered Most." I hope the stories of Virginia Hall, James Armistead Lafayette, Sybil Ludington, and the other hidden heroes inspired you as much as they inspired me while writing this book.

These forgotten patriots prove that ordinary people can do extraordinary things when their country needs them most. Their courage shaped America, and their examples can guide us today.

Your Review Matters

If this book moved you, educated you, or changed how you think about American heroism, would you consider leaving a review on Amazon?

Your honest feedback helps other readers discover these important stories and ensures that these hidden heroes finally receive the recognition they deserve.

Scan the QR code above or search "The Secret Patriots" on Amazon

Whether you give it 5 stars or fewer, your authentic response helps spread these crucial stories to people who need to hear them.

The Story Continues

Remember: heroism isn't reserved for special people in special times. The same courage that drove these secret patriots lives within ordinary Americans today including you.

Thank you for taking this journey through hidden history. Now go change the world.

With gratitude,

Grant Whitmore

P.S. - *If you know someone who would be inspired by these stories, please share this book with them. Democracy depends on citizens who understand that they have the power to make a difference.*

www.ingramcontent.com/pod-product-compliance
Lightning Source LLC
Chambersburg PA
CBHW071146070526
44584CB00019B/2675